WRITING HANDBOOKS

Writing
FANTASY &
SCIENCE FICTION

SECOND EDITION

D0642931

WRITING HANDBOOKS

Writing
FANTASY &
SCIENCE FICTION

SECOND EDITION

LISA TUTTLE

A & C Black • London

To George RR
everywhere in these pages

Second edition 2005
First published 2001
A & C Black Publishers Limited
37 Soho Square, London W1D 3QZ
www.acblack.com

© 2005, 2001 Lisa Tuttle

ISBN 0–7136–7244–7

A CIP catalogue record for this book is
available from the British Library.

A & C Black uses paper produced with elemental chlorine-free pulp,
harvested from managed sustainable forests.

Typeset in 10.5/13.5 pt Sabon
Printed and bound in Great Britain by
Creative Print and Design (Wales), Ebbw Vale

Contents

1
Staking Out the Territory

Most of the skills you need for writing fantasy or science fiction are the same as for any other sort of fiction. A good story, believable characters and a fluent, readable style are absolutely vital to all saleable popular fiction – whether thriller, romance, fantasy or science fiction. Whatever your other strengths and interests as a writer, you must be strong in all the basics of good fiction in order to succeed.

People who don't read fantasy may dismiss it as 'unreal'. Because it's not bound by the restrictions of ordinary reality, they assume that 'anything goes' and it must therefore be particularly easy to write. In Joanne Harris's *Blackberry Wine* the protagonist, a one-time literary star, finds himself blocked and unable to write 'serious' novels, yet manages to make a living by bashing out pseudonymous fantasy novels. I enjoyed the novel (a fantasy itself, I might point out!) but the idea that fantasy is somehow not 'real' writing is, frankly, fantastic.

Science fiction as a genre is often considered especially difficult, requiring specialist abilities not only to write, but also to read it. In a densely argued critical essay, Samuel R. Delany has demonstrated that in science fiction, what he calls the 'level of subjunctivity' is distinctly different, on a word-by-word basis, from that in naturalistic fiction. Both science fiction and fantasy require a constant awareness that the reality of the story is different from the reader's own reality. That's why, for some readers, this genre is very hard work.

It requires hard work from the writer, too, but if you're already a science fiction or fantasy reader, you should have some idea of what's involved, consider it an exciting challenge rather than an impossible task, and, most importantly, know that this is the sort of fiction you most want to write.

One genre, or two?

As a marketing category, fantasy and science fiction tend to be grouped together. They are published under one imprint, usually purchased by the same editor, and are displayed in a special section in bookshops and libraries, separate from other genre categories such as romance or crime.

Although some fantasy readers dislike the futuristic and technological slant of science fiction, and some hardcore science fiction fans despise fantasy, many readers enjoy both. Generalisations can be made about the differences between the two types of fiction, yet individual works may be hard to classify, and there's no hard-and-fast dividing line that distinguishes all science fiction from all fantasy. Both tell stories about things that don't exist, in contrast to 'realistic' fiction which is supposed to deal with the world as it really is. Fantasy is the larger, wider and older field, since it includes folktales and fairy tales as well as the modern subset known as science fiction.

A lot of time and effort has been spent by fans and critics in trying to come up with an elegant and satisfying definition of science fiction. I don't want to get caught up in that particular struggle here, so I hope it will be enough to say that, in general, science fiction tends to be about things which are theoretically possible – or at least not known to be impossible. By contrast, fantasy encompasses the impossible. In fantasies, magic works; it doesn't have to be explained. Instead of the wizardly powers, enchanted realms and strange beasts of fantasy, science fiction features awesome machines, distant planets, and wonders created by science and advanced technology.

Some writers are primarily identified with one specific genre (heroic fantasy for Robert Jordan, hard science fiction for Stephen Baxter), while others, like Ursula LeGuin and Samuel Delany, move back and forth between fantasy and science fiction. There are distinctions between the genres which are recognised by readers, even if they're not easily defined, yet some books can't be neatly categorised: for example, *Perdido Street Station* by China Mieville is set in a fantasy world with the 'feel' of science fiction, and *Ash: A Secret History* by Mary Gentle is set in an alternative 15th century and the present day. Both novels were nominated for different 'Best Science Fiction Novel' and 'Best Fantasy Novel' awards in 2000–2001.

The same book may be described as science fiction, fantasy, literary fiction, horror, futuristic thriller, or magical realism, depending on the expected audience, current state of the market or a critic's particular prejudices. Describing books in terms of genre has more to do with convenience and marketing than it does with prescriptions for how to write. Most of what I have to say in this book about writing will apply to most fiction. When fantasy or science fiction have specific requirements, I'll spell them out.

Why write science fiction (SF)?

A note about terminology

'Sci-fi' is a popular short-hand term for science fiction, but I don't like it. In the 1970s and 1980s, people who said 'sci-fi' almost invariably didn't read it. The preferred term among writers and fans was – and generally still is – SF (or sf). This abbreviation is neat, classic, doesn't raise questions about pronunciation (shouldn't 'sci-fi' be pronounced 'skiffy'?) and has the additional benefit of being open to alternative interpretations. Thus, if you think 'science fiction' sounds too limited (fiction about science?), SF can stand for speculative fiction, science fantasy, space fiction, or speculative fantasy.

Most SF writers are SF readers first. They are drawn to this genre perhaps by an interest in science, technology, or the future. They tend to have a rational, questioning approach to things.

SF is above all a literature of ideas, of wonder and speculation. 'Speculative fiction' has been proposed as a more appropriate term than 'science fiction' because SF writers frequently speculate about the future. They ask, 'What will happen if *this* goes on?' *This* may be anything – fashion trends, genetic engi-

3

neering, the expansion of big business, the use of the Internet, creeping socialism, exploding capitalism, a drop in church attendance, an increase in the birth rate, the popularity of quiz shows on TV... And they ask, 'What if...?' What if someone built a working time machine? What if an immortality treatment became available? What if an advanced race of beings made contact with us? What if a new plague wiped out more than half the earth's population? What if a comet hit the earth tomorrow?

If questions like those spark your imagination, if you like to make imaginative leaps and then carefully work out the likely, realistic consequences that might arise, then SF may be for you. But do read a lot of it before you try to write it. Colin Murray, who has worked as an editor in this field for nearly 30 years, once told me that many of the worst SF novels he'd rejected over the years were written by people who'd clearly never read any science fiction. If you don't read it, you won't know that your 'new idea' was first explored in 1918, or that half a dozen novels have been published on the same subject within the last three years. Your 'surprise' ending might have worked in 1962, but by now it is probably a well-worn cliché. If you haven't read much SF, you won't know if you are struggling to reinvent the wheel. Although it's good to read the classics, it's probably even more important to be aware of what contemporary SF writers are doing now. So if you used to read SF as a kid but haven't done so since, take the time to bring yourself up to date with the writers of today.

It's not enough for a writer to be familiar with SF through films and television alone. SF novels and stories are often aimed at a more sophisticated, informed audience than mass-market television. On the screen, illogical plots may be disguised by special effects, or redeemed by the actors. On the page, mistakes, omissions and shortcuts are glaringly obvious.

Not everyone likes SF. If you have contempt for the genre – or for the audience that enjoys it – you shouldn't try to write it. Don't make the mistake of thinking that you can write something good without caring about it, or that your brilliant ideas matter more than good plotting and believable characters, or that style is a substitute for substance. SF requires the same skills as any other fiction – and then some.

If you love to read about science, if you want to explore the impact of new technologies on peoples' lives, if you like to think about the future, explore metaphysical and ethical questions, invent new societies, imagine the outcome of current trends, and aren't afraid of doing research – maybe you should write science fiction.

The cold equations

However, if you're hoping to make a living from writing, you might do better to consider something else. SF is a rather specialised field, requiring a lot of work and commitment to do well, and monetary rewards don't always follow. In fact, if money is your major goal, better to steer away from writing altogether!

A survey conducted by the Society of Authors among its membership in 2000 revealed that 75% of the respondents earned less than the national average wage; and half earned less than an employee on the national *minimum* wage. Even worse, 46% had earned under £5,000 from their writing in the previous year. The survey also showed that genre fiction writers (except for mystery and thriller writers) were especially badly off, and the most likely to find the sizes of their advances going down. Yet, based on Public Lending Right payments, genre fiction, including SF, continues to be widely read, and is especially popular with library users. And if you manage to write a book that truly speaks to our dreams and fears about the rapidly changing world around us, like the SF classics of the past, you could become one of the bright new stars of the future.

Types of science fiction

The following are only a few of the most obvious and popular types of SF. Many SF novels contain a variety of elements and are not easily sorted into sub-classifications.

Hard SF

Hard SF takes as its basis established – or carefully extrapolated – scientific knowledge. It tends to concentrate on 'hard' sciences such as physics, engineering, astronomy, cosmology and cybernetics, rather than on 'soft' sciences like anthropology, psychology or sociology. There is usually an emphasis on hardware, like spaceships, computers and weapons. Sometimes it ventures into futurology, attempting to predict ways in which scientific advances may change or improve our lives. Even when it moves well beyond what we know to be possible, hard SF is always grounded in fact and theory, and expects the reader to share a rational, scientific attitude towards the universe.

Space opera

The film *Star Wars*, modelled on old-fashioned movie serials, is a classic example of space opera – colourful, fast-moving, melodramatic adventures which take place aboard spaceships and on alien planets, set in the far future usually against the background of some sort of intergalactic empire. There may be a background based on hard, scientific extrapolation, or it may be a form of fantasy given intergalactic settings. Colin Greenland's *Take Back Plenty* is a good example, as are the Culture novels of Iain M. Banks, and Lois McMaster Bujold's series about the Vor Empire.

Military SF

This may be more or less 'hard' and may have some affinities with space opera, but the emphasis is on warfare, the tactics of fighting, and military life and protocol in the future, in space, and on other worlds – with political theory often of more concern than any of the physical sciences. David Drake's *Hammer's Slammers* sequence and his *Northworld* series are examples, as are books by David Feintuch and Elizabeth Moon.

Cyberpunk

This term, coined in the 1980s, referred to an emerging strand of SF novels which seized on ideas about virtual reality and new information technology, the merging of machine and human, the development of artificial intelligence, and a changing political scene which saw true power moving away from governments and towards transnational corporations. The most famous of the original 'cyberpunk' writers are William Gibson – his classic *Neuromancer* has inspired many imitators – and Bruce Sterling. Other writers who have written in a similar vein include Eric Brown, Michael Marshall Smith, and Pat Cadigan. Visually, films such as *The Matrix* and many computer games are indebted to the cyberpunk style, although it is now perceived as somewhat old-fashioned.

Steampunk

This is a rather jokey term created by analogy with 'cyberpunk' and used to describe a subgenre of SF set not in the future, like most SF, but in an alternative past. *The Difference Engine* by Bruce Sterling and William Gibson postulates the invention of the computer in pre-Victorian times and imagines a 19th-century London on the verge of collapse. James Blaylock, K.W. Jeter and Tim Powers have also written novels set in an imaginary past, and a similar feeling is found in works by China Mieville and Neal Stephenson.

Alternate realities

These may be in the past, present or future. Because of the 'many worlds' theory postulated by Niels Bohr to explain what physicist Richard Feynman once called 'the only mystery' in physics, some stories set in 'secondary worlds' should be considered science fiction rather than fantasy. In Philip K. Dick's *The Man in the High Castle*, half of America is dominated by Nazis, while the other half is occupied by the Japanese. Mary Gentle's *Ash: A Secret History* concerns the gradual discovery, in our present day, of a fault-line in history – a moment in the 15th century when everything changed. My own *Lost Futures* explores the 'many worlds' theory through alternative versions of one person's life. Although experiments carried out by Shahriar S. Afshar in 2004 appear to have debunked the 'many worlds' theory in scientific circles, it seems likely to continue to be popular with science fiction writers.

Thrillers

Near-future thrillers, in which an important element of the plot relies on plausible scientific advances or discoveries, and their unintended terrifying consequences, are perhaps the type of science fiction most likely to make it into the bestseller lists. They are usually set no more than a few years ahead – 'the day after tomorrow' – in a recognisably contemporary world, with a fast-moving, suspenseful storyline. They often dramatise ideas that are just beginning to impinge on the public consciousness, and exploit fears about how people and society may be changed by new technologies. Michael Crichton is particularly successful in this realm.

Utopias and dystopias

For utopia, authors try to imagine and describe the 'perfect state'. Because perfection tends to lack drama, a straightforward utopia could be dull; therefore, utopias in science fiction are usually represented as being under threat, or are set in contrast to a world that is much worse than our own – a dystopia. There is a strong tradition in science fiction of presenting a dystopian future as the result of some contemporary trend (e.g. pollution, consumerism, religious fundamentalism) carried to an horrendous extreme. The Culture novels of Iain M. Banks are anarcho-socialist utopias; Ursula LeGuin's *The Dispossessed* is sub-titled 'An Ambiguous Utopia', and presents two different notions of 'success'. In Marge Piercy's *Woman on the Edge of Time*, an egalitarian, sexually liberated future is contrasted with the miserable daily life of a poor woman prisoner in our world.

Why write fantasy?

At first glance, fantasy seems a better bet than science fiction for the ambitious beginner. J. K. Rowling was a complete unknown when her first novel, *Harry Potter and the Philosopher's Stone*, was accepted for publication; within a few years, she was a worldwide bestseller. Other fantasy writers – Terry Pratchett, David and Leigh Eddings, Robert Jordan – regularly hit the bestseller lists and have hordes of fans eagerly awaiting their latest publications. J. R. R. Tolkien's books continue to sell in great numbers half a century after they were written, and his trilogy *The Lord of the Rings* was voted the book of the century after a BBC-sponsored campaign to find the nation's favourite read.

Yet it is worth pointing out that nobody can predict what will become a bestseller. J. R. R. Tolkien didn't begin his life's work of creating an imaginary world with any notion of becoming rich and famous; he wrote (and painted) for his own pleasure, and for that of a very small audience. Although his books attracted a cultish following, their popularity built over decades. Similarly, it took years for Terry Pratchett's books to catch on. Although he sold his first novel in 1971, it was not until 1987 that he felt secure enough in his earnings as a writer to quit his regular job. Even J. K. Rowling was not an overnight success.

The best reason for writing fantasy is the same reason for writing anything: because you feel you have to, because you love it, because you have a story to tell.

Although it is increasingly popular these days, fantasy doesn't appeal to everyone. Many readers prefer their fiction to reflect the world they see around them, with people like themselves falling in love, getting married, being betrayed, getting divorced, drinking too much, and maybe, just maybe, winning the lottery. That's about as far as they want their imaginations to stretch. As for witches, unicorns and wild sorcery in another realm – forget it!

Not all fantasy writers read a lot of genre fantasy. People who write fantasy find their imaginations stirred by the strange and impossible. They may find ordinary life rather dull; they may be attracted to exotic travel and the study of history or comparative religions. They certainly read a lot. What they read *may* include a lot of fantasy, but not necessarily.

J. R. R. Tolkien, who wrote the prototype of the modern fantasy novel, might be said to have founded the contemporary genre. He was inspired by his studies in Anglo-Saxon and early forms of English, and by his wide readings in mythology. In a radio interview, Philip Pullman said that he didn't like fantasy. In his opinion, most books labelled 'fantasy' were not about anything real – and although he'd set his *His Dark Materials* trilogy in an imaginary world containing magic, daemons and witches, he did so in order to write about real emotions and concerns. He was inspired not by books about elves and magic rings, but by Milton's *Paradise Lost* and the art and writings of William Blake.

There is no need to 'study' fantasy before attempting to write it – as long as you have a good grounding in literature. You don't have to believe in magic or ghosts to write about them, as long as you take them seriously, and treat your readership with respect. It's a good idea to read *some* contemporary fantasy, however, if this is the field you hope to excel in. Reading the most popular current titles will make you aware of general trends, reader expectations, and what sells – as well as educating you in current clichés, so you can avoid repeating them.

A regular marketing ploy with publishers is to identify a new writer as being 'in the tradition of' Tolkien, Jordan, McCaffrey, Rowling, etc. But second-hand imitations are never very successful. Avoid modelling yourself on another writer, no matter how much you admire their work. Writers may be aware of working within a tradition, but the best of them try to break away. They will put their own distinctive stamp on their material, working hard to create their own worlds, rather than simply moving into one imagined by others.

Types of fantasy

The literature of the fantastic covers a lot of ground, including the gothic, ghost stories, horror fiction, mythology, fairy tales, surrealism and modern 'magical realism'. However, most books labelled 'fantasy' are set beyond our daily reality, in what may be called a 'secondary world'. This term was coined by J. R. R.

Tolkien in a 1939 lecture, 'On Fairy Tales', and his Middle Earth is a prime example of a secondary world. Tolkien is undoubtedly the most famous, and influential, of all fantasy writers. Prior to Tolkien, writers tended to explain their imaginary worlds by carefully locating them in regard to our own: adventurers might reach one by falling down a rabbit-hole, flying to another planet, or travelling to some distant lost valley. Alternatively the fantasy adventure would turn out to be a dream, or something which happened long, long ago. Since the publication of *The Lord of the Rings*, however, fantasy writers have felt free to present stories set in a totally imaginary world without explanation or apology. Some sort of magic is usually at work in this imaginary world, but its importance varies. In many fantasies, supernatural powers are crucial to the plot, while in others magic hardly features at all. There may be monsters or mythical beasts, and the social structure is usually based on something other than modern democracy; often it is a rigidly hierarchical society, represented as being at a low level of technological development.

Not all fantasies fit neatly into one subgenre or another, but I'll describe a few of the most obvious below.

Heroic fantasy

Also known as 'sword and sorcery', this concerns the adventures of a hero (or heroine) attempting to survive – often, to complete a series of tasks or to find something in a quest. Examples include the *Conan* stories by Robert E. Howard and others; Fritz Leiber's *Fahfrd and the Gray Mouser* books; and the *Alyx* adventures by Joanna Russ.

Epic or high fantasy

This has a close affinity to heroic fantasy; the main difference is that the longer, epic fantasies put less emphasis on the hero-figure. Instead, there will be a larger cast of important characters, and the main protagonist is likely to be an ordinary person, whom no one would consider heroic – like Bilbo Baggins, in *The Hobbit*, and his cousin Frodo in *The Lord of the Rings*.

Dynastic fantasies

These are an outgrowth of epic or heroic fantasy. They take place over many years and fill a series of books as the descendants of the original hero fight among themselves to achieve leadership, or against some mighty, supernatural enemy determined to destroy whatever the original hero fought to find or preserve. The *Belgariad* series by David Eddings is an example, as is George R.R. Martin's *A Song of Ice and Fire*.

Humorous fantasy

A very popular genre, but hard to do well. Parodies work only if they are sharp (and, generally, short) and if the readership is very familiar with what is being parodied. To be really successful, the humorous fantasist needs to go beyond simple parody, to combine comedy and inventiveness with a well-told story that works on its own terms. Terry Pratchett is undoubtedly the star in this field – in fact, it could be said that he has created a genre all his own. His *Discworld* novels continue to grow in popularity, and appeal to people who read a lot of fantasy as well as to those who don't.

Dark fantasy

Sometimes used as a more 'respectable' term for supernatural horror fiction, but also describes fantasies such as Stephen Donaldson's *Covenant* series in which a brooding sense of horror pervades the story, and vampire books like Kim Newman's funny and inventive *Anno Dracula* series. In general, occult, ghost and supernatural stories are considered 'horror' rather than 'fantasy' for marketing purposes.

Magic realism

The posh end of fantasy, usually published as mainstream, literary fiction. Among its strengths are fine writing and fascinating characters; the plot may concern an inexplicable intrusion of the magical or otherworldly into otherwise ordinary lives. Examples can be found in the works of Angela Carter, Gabriel Garcia Marquez, and Alice Hoffman among others.

Time-slip fantasies

In these, characters from one era travel through time to have adventures in another. Time-slip fantasies may be published as science fiction (like Robert Adams' *Castaways in Time* series or Jack Finney's *Time and Again*). Alternatively, they may be marketed as romance, as with Diana Gabaldon's *Outlander* series.

Romantic fantasy

This is aimed at a predominantly female readership, and has developed recently into a new subgenre in the United States. In 2004, Harlequin – a brand-name for popular category romances – set up a list called Luna to publish science fiction and fantasy with strong feminine appeal; in the same year Tor established a 'Paranormal Romance' programme that includes science fiction, fantasy, horror, time travel and alternate history in which a romantic storyline is crucial to the novel. Writers of romantic fantasy (and SF) include Laura Anne Gilman, Sarah Zettel and Catherine Asaro. Additionally, writers better known for genre romance have started using fantasy elements in contemporary settings – for example, the 'Key' trilogy by bestselling author Nora Roberts.

Shared worlds and tie-ins

The publication of media tie-ins – that is, books connected in some way to films and TV series – has more than doubled over the past 20 years. Judging by statistics published annually in *Locus* magazine, media tie-ins now comprise almost 20% of all science fiction and fantasy books published. These include novelisations of scripts as well as 'spin-offs' – series of original novels about characters from the various *Star Trek* series or the *Star Wars* movies, or from *Men In Black* (the movies and television cartoon series are both based on an original comic book), or *Buffy the Vampire Slayer*, or almost any other popular SF, fantasy or horror title – and many of them sell extremely well, even hitting the bestseller lists. The rights to the characters and their 'world' are generally owned by production companies who license their publication and hold the copyright. Authors are commissioned by the publisher, usually receiving an advance and a share of royalties (split with the copyright-owner) for their work, but occasionally being offered only a flat fee, known as 'work for hire'.

In the past, this was poorly paid work, but these days there is a lot more money in it. Sometimes the author's job is to 'novelise' a script – that is, to take the actual script of the film or TV show as the outline for a novel, fleshing it out with descriptions, additional scenes and dialogue to get it up to the required length. The amount of imaginative freedom that they are allowed for this varies. For spin-off series, however, authors are asked to write original novels. They're usually given a so-called 'bible' or 'almanac' containing important details about major and minor characters and the background of their universe. Then, much as if they were writing scripts for the series, the author writes a novel utilising the established background and characters.

Books of this sort are written on commission, by permission of the copyright-holder. There is no point in deciding you'll launch your career with a novel about Dr Who, or one set in the *Star Wars* universe, no matter how much you love the characters nor how great your ideas are, because you won't be allowed to publish it. Publishers tend not to commission previously unpublished writers to write tie-in novels, either. Your best bet, if this type of writing appeals to you, is to write your own original work based on your own ideas and characters, get it published, and then, with at least one published novel on your CV, let your agent and publisher know that you'd be interested in writing novelisations. A number of SF and fantasy writers manage to make a good living as full-time writers, by working in other people's universes in this way.

Another type of shared-world writing is when a writer allows other writers to make use of their own imaginary world – as when Marion Zimmer Bradley invited other writers to write their own stories set in her invented world of Darkover, or when Neil Gaiman asked other writers to contribute their own stories about his popular comic-book character, the Sandman. Other shared worlds include Isaac Asimov's Robot City, Andre Norton's Witch World, and Fred Saberhagen's *Berserker* series.

Occasionally, SF and fantasy worlds are shared from the very start, when groups of writers invent them together as a form of collaboration. Rather than a series of novels, the result is usually one or more anthologies, sometimes invitational, sometimes open to all-comers – for example, the *Wild Cards* series originated by George R. R. Martin and friends.

Crossover books

A buzzword in publishing circles is the 'crossover' – also known as a 'breakout' book. Books seen as having crossover or break-out potential are those which an editor believes will appeal to more than a single genre's readership. It could hook both fantasy readers and romance readers (like Diana Gabaldon's *Outlander* series), or transcend its genre entirely by becoming a bestseller (like Terry Pratchett). However, be warned that SF and fantasy are not considered separate genres. Combining SF with fantasy will irritate some readers and cause fans to argue over definitions, but the resultant book will be shelved in the same place and aimed at the same audience whether it is labelled 'fantasy', 'science fiction' or 'science fantasy'.

More recently, the crossover book that has become the holy grail of publishing is the novel which will appeal to children and adults alike: the Harry Potter books have led the way here, of course.

The downside of writing a book which crosses genre – or age – boundaries is that it may not be seen as a potential huge success, but instead as a book which fits no single obvious category and is therefore 'unmarketable'. I know of more than one good book that met such a fate in recent years. If you've written a novel which doesn't 'fit' an editor's list, you have my sympathy. My advice is to get on with writing your next book – but not to give up hope on your misfit. Fashions change, as do categories, and editors. Eventually, there may be a place for it, or an editor may like it enough to take a risk. Who knows? Your uncategorisable book may launch a whole new genre.

The right length

Ideally, a book is as long as it has to be. A story should define its own length.

Any work of fiction over 40,000 words long is considered to be a novel. However, in practical terms, most SF and fantasy editors would consider a book of fewer than 60,000 words to be 'too short'. The length of the average SF novel these days may be anything between 80,000 and 150,000 words.

It is unusual for a commercial fantasy novel to be fewer than 100,000 words; casting an eye over some recently published fantasies, I'd say that 200,000 to 300,000 words is not uncommon – and some are even longer than that. George R. R. Martin's *A Storm of Swords*, the third in his *A Song of Ice and Fire* sequence, ran to 1,521 pages in manuscript – well over 500,000 words. The fact that Mary Gentle's *Ash: A Secret History* ran to 1,113 pages in the British hardback edition probably has something to do with why it's regarded by some as fantasy rather than science fiction.

For practical reasons, publishers aren't happy about publishing books of 1,000 pages or more. They're more expensive, and difficult to produce in an attractive, readable, durable format. Big, heavy hardbacks are bad enough, but overweight paperbacks are likely to fall apart during the first reading.

My personal taste is for short novels, but I know that this is unusual: I've been told by agents and editors that readers today prefer big, hefty books. Just as fast-food outlets exhort us to 'Go Large!', and supermarkets offer a 'free' 30% more to attract customers, it seems that publishers, too, feel that book-buyers expect more wordage for their money.

Certain subgenres like the epic or dynastic fantasy obviously require a large scale to be effective, and for most readers the appeal of the secondary world is as a place to live, in imagination, for many days or weeks. For those readers, one single novel is never enough. Thanks to the immense popularity of J. R. R. Tolkien's *The Lord of the Rings*, the idea that the trilogy – three volumes – was the natural format for that sort of book took hold. As a result, too many junior would-be Tolkiens have pulled and stretched their 'epics' to fill three fat books when they might have done better to write one.

There is no 'normal' length for a fantasy novel; one size does not fit all, and whether some fantasy series have continued well past their best is a matter for fans and critics to argue over.

Sometimes, after lovingly creating a world for one novel, the author can't bear to leave it and begins thinking of more stories to tell within it. However, it is probably more usual for a series to be conceived as such from the beginning. J. K. Rowling seems to have intended for there to be seven Harry Potter adventures even before she'd sold the first one. I think that George R. R. Martin still plans for *A Song of Ice and Fire* to run to six volumes, but as each subsequent book has been longer than the last, I wonder if nine or 12 might not prove a more realistic estimate.

Writing a book that is meant to stretch over several volumes – which won't be published all at once – raises certain problems that the author of a self-contained novel does not face. In the first place, each individual book must be a satisfying read on its own. Although the end of Book One should leave the reader eager for more, it must not disappoint, nor feel unfinished. Some questions can be left unanswered, and plot threads unresolved, but the reader should always feel rewarded – and all the more so if the sequel won't be published for another year or more.

With a sequel, even though most readers will have read the first volume, authors writing their second book can't take their knowledge of what went before for granted. A sequel has to attract new readers as well, so it must be approachable, comprehensible, and enjoyable as a stand-alone novel. Certain things will have to be repeated, and explanations given for those who've forgotten, or haven't read, the first book, and this must be done in a way that will amuse rather than bore or irritate those readers who've picked it up immediately after Book One. Writing and integrating such material takes a very particular skill.

Never try to pad out your story to make it longer simply because you think it 'should' be long in order to sell. If the material and the treatment don't justify the length – if the story simply meanders along, filling up pages but going nowhere – no one will appreciate whatever strengths it might have beneath all those words. It may be true that book-buyers want bulk, but hay will not satisfy them when they're looking for meat. All stories are not equally interesting. Some ideas work best as short stories, and some require a long, slow development. With practice, you'll learn to let your ideas dictate their own best length.

2
Ideas and Archetypes

Science fiction is often described as a 'literature of ideas'. Whereas fantasy tends to look back to traditional patterns and age-old stories, science fiction strives for originality. It tends, like all genre fiction, to be plot-driven, but people do expect something more than just a good story when they read SF. Often, they want to be challenged intellectually, to be made to think about things which are far outside the bounds of ordinary daily life. Novelty and inventiveness are highly prized. Sometimes claims are made that science fiction 'predicts' the future; but it is not a branch of futurology, and SF writers are no more accurate in their 'predictions' than anyone else. Most SF writers aren't actually trying to predict what *will* happen in the future – only to consider what *might*. Some writers use SF to create 'thought-experiments', testing out in fiction things which can't be explored in real life. SF is often about change. It explores the impact of progress on individuals and on societies.

Ask questions

What is it that makes us human? How might future technology change the world and our relationship to it and to each other? How could society be redesigned to make life more fair? How would people act if they were immortal? If they were cloned? If the body were no more significant than a suit of clothes?

Think of your favourite SF novels or stories. What makes them outstanding? They may be well-written, they may tell a good story, but chances are that what you remember best about them are the ideas. Some of my favourites are: the gestalt mind

19

of Theodore Sturgeon's *More Than Human*; Rydra Wong's tele-pathy in Samuel R. Delany's *Babel-17*; the concept of memory as something to be bought and sold, a drug that alters not only perception but also reality, a world in which time flows back-wards, and other bizarre and powerful notions from the writings of Philip K. Dick; the depiction of the subconscious mind as a separate entity in Kate Wilhelm's *Margaret and I*; Ursula LeGuin's exploration of a world without gender in *The Left Hand of Darkness*; and the intelligent, consciousness-trans-forming disease of Greg Bear's *Blood Music*.

Whether the authors 'invented' these ideas, or were the first to use them, isn't significant. It's *how* they used them, clothed them in story and made them live, which matters. Often a number of writers are drawn to explore the same ideas at the same time, because these are questions which are very much in the public consciousness, and in the news. Writers may con-sciously borrow ideas from books they've read, wanting to argue or put their own spin on them, or they may absorb them unconsciously from the common culture. Ideas get recycled, reused, and some become such common currency within SF that their origins are forgotten. Some popular fictional concepts can become as widely accepted as actual facts.

Fact or fiction?

Cyberspace. This word is often used to refer to computer-generated virtual realities, as well as to the 'location' of anything on the Internet. As a space, it doesn't exist – yet we discuss it as if it did.

The term cyberspace was invented by William Gibson for his 1984 novel, *Neuromancer*. In his fiction, cyberspace was a 'consensual hallucination' of his near-future world; a global information network (rather like the worldwide web which was then only in its infancy) which could be accessed directly by human brains through neural implants plugged into computers. We still don't have those neural implants in reality, yet they are a commonplace in fiction now. Gibson's vision has been hugely influential on other writers – the image of plugged-in hackers roaming virtual space has been incorporated into many subsequent visions of the future – yet even he didn't invent it entirely from scratch: the idea of cyborgs (human/machine hybrids) had been around in science fiction for decades.

Robots are another example. The word 'robot' first appeared in the play *R.U.R.* by Czech author Karel Capek, in 1921. Capek's 'robots' (the word came from the Czech *robota*, meaning compulsory labour) were actually artifical but organic human beings, which would more usually be called 'androids' in later science fiction. The term 'robot' was transferred to a type of machine, both in fiction and in reality. Capek didn't invent the *idea* of the robot, but he gave the idea a new name. Clockwork dolls and animated puppets had been invented more than a century earlier, and the notion of artificially created servants can be traced back much, much earlier in folktale and legend. The Golem, for example, in Hebrew legend, was a man of clay brought to life by words of power written down and inserted into its mouth by the master who controlled it.

Where do ideas come from?

Tired of the eternal question faced by writers everywhere – 'Where do you get your ideas?' – Harlan Ellison developed a whole fantasy riff on the subject. They come from Schenectady, he'd say. Yeah, that's right, Schenectady, New York. It's a service. No, I won't give you the address, but all the professional writers know about it – how else could we keep churning out the work? For a modest monthly fee, we get a regular supply of brilliant ideas, arriving in the mail in a plain brown envelope ...

There's a mystique around the concept of the 'great idea' which reflects the desire for quick, magical solutions. People want to believe that there's a secret to success, some sort of hidden treasure which *anyone* can access, if only ... This attitude is more common in Hollywood, where 'high concept' (obvious ideas which can be explained in one line) is more saleable than 'low concept' (those which can't). Getting an idea is like buying a lottery ticket – it's not difficult, and it's just about as likely to make you rich.

There is no single, magical source of ideas – except your own mind. The raw material for them is everywhere, in the life around us. Only when an individual responds to something – an image, a pattern of events, an arrangement of words in a song, a newspaper headline, an emotion – is that something singled out and transformed into 'an idea for a story'. The development of idea from notion to story is really what it's all about.

What triggers one person's excitement may seem meaningless to someone else. And three different writers will bring three different interpretations to the 'same idea', whether their starting point is dragons as pets, an alien invasion, or the discovery of an immortality gene. Anyone who's ever done writing exercises as part of a class, judged a writing competition, or read two-dozen essays on the same subject will know that although certain clichés, and the same lazy shortcuts and mistakes will turn up again and again, every individual sees the world in a slightly different way. Writers do get nervous whenever they hear that another writer has tackled a subject the same as their own, but fiction isn't biography or travel writing. Ben Bova's 'Mars' isn't Paul McAuley's or Kim Stanley Robinson's ... not to mention Ray Bradbury's or Edgar Rice Burroughs' or Robert Heinlein's red planet.

The source

I can't tell you where other people get their ideas from (except that Harlan gets his from Schenectady), but I can track the sources of most of my own. Here are a few:

'The Cure' was triggered by the headline of an interview with William S. Burroughs. It said something like, 'Language is a Virus'. I don't think I actually read the article, but that statement lodged in my mind. What if it really were, I thought, and what if in our relentless crusade to wipe out disease, this ancient virus lurking in our DNA were to be destroyed, and humanity 'cured' of language? To this day I don't know what point Burroughs was making. Maybe he meant it as an analogy, or a metaphor – language 'infects' people or 'spreads' like a virus? All I can say is that the conjunction of those two words – the idea of language as a (benevolent?) disease – fired my imagination, and I was especially intrigued by the technical challenge: how could I capture the point of view of someone for whom words had become meaningless? How would it feel to be a person without language?

My very first professional sale, 'Stranger in the House', had quite a different starting point. At first, I had no ideas at all – just the wish to write a scary story. So I searched my memory for things that had scared me as a kid. I remembered how I used to run across the room and leap onto the bed, pulling my legs out of the way of anything that might be underneath it and try to grab them. Although I never had a mental image of what sort of monster might be lurking there, and often hid there myself in games of hide-and-seek, at bedtime it seemed like a dangerous place. Beginning the story with the memory of my mysterious fear, and trying to come up with a convincing danger that might lurk under the bed, I used the fact that I was staying in a strange city and feeling a little homesick to create my main character – a youngish woman unhappy in her present life and determined somehow to make her way back to the childhood where she'd had last felt comfortable and at home.

'The Family Monkey', the tale of a West Texas family with an alien in their midst, was inspired by what I thought was a true story. In 1897, the western US was baffled by a rash of 'airship' appearances, like a precursor of the UFO flap of the 1950s. One of these airships supposedly crashed near a small Texas town, and an 'inhuman' body was found inside and buried in the local graveyard. (Much later, I read that this was a hoax devised to boost the circulation of a Dallas newspaper.) I wondered what might have happened if a living, though damaged, inhuman creature had been rescued by a ranching family, and explored

23

the situation by developing my small cast of characters. I never worked out a plot, just thought about what they might do. Encountering a poem called 'The Family Monkey' by Russell Edson at around the same time gave me both the title and the emotional ambiance of the story.

Mad House was sparked by a newspaper article about a 'smart fridge' which would be able to order whatever you needed without being told. I immediately began to think of all the things that could go wrong in a house full of super-smart machines – and because I wanted to write a story for young readers, I kept it on a lightly humorous level, aiming for a comforting, rather than terrifying, conclusion.

Some of these ideas may be familiar to you. Except for language is a virus – which was William Burroughs' idea, not mine – they are all old standards in the SF/fantasy field, and the only originality I can claim is in my own style and approach. Looking back on 'Stranger in the House', I can see how influenced I was by Ray Bradbury's yearning nostalgia for childhood; I was also well aware, from countless SF stories, that the time-traveller returning to his own past runs the risk of deadly paradox: how can there be more than one of you? *Mad House* had such towering precursors as Arthur C. Clarke's and Stanley Kubrick's *2001: A Space Odyssey*, Harlan Ellison's 'I Have No Mouth and I Must Scream', and Dean Koontz's *Demon Seed* in the idea of a trapped machine intelligence interacting with and victimising mere humans.

Arguing with others

New concepts are highly prized in our culture, but they are hard to come by. Even in Biblical times it was said, 'There is no new thing under the sun.'

Many writers, myself included, have written stories directly inspired by other stories. SF is a genre in an ongoing conversation with itself. Certain topics come up again and again; some cause fierce arguments. Sometimes, stories that annoy can be of more use to the writer than those that are perfectly enjoyable.

Joanna Russ wrote *We Who Are About To* ... in argument with the standard SF idea that a group of people stranded on a distant, uninhabited planet had a moral imperative to colonise it. Among other books, she was responding to Marion Zimmer Bradley's *Darkover Landfall*, and the idea that women's first – and joyful! – duty is to reproduce the species. By contrast with the other seven survivors, all determined to 'preserve civilisation' by making every woman of reproductive age pregnant, the (mature, female) narrator of *We Who Are About To* ... questions the desireability of struggling against the odds to prolong the sort of primitive life they can expect.

Two stories of mine, 'The Wound' and 'Lizard Lust', were written in response to Ursula LeGuin's *The Left Hand of Darkness* – a novel that she has described as having written, at least in part, to explore the question of how people might live and behave if fixed biological gender were not established at birth.

Myths and archetypes

Fantasy, too, asks 'What if ...?' and imagines a world different from our own, but is distinguished from science fiction in that its point of departure doesn't have to be possible or logical. Fantasy could never be confused with an attempt to predict or prescribe, as SF occasionally is. Fantasy is concerned with other realities, not logical extensions of our present. Rather than inventing the future, as SF does, fantasy reimagines the past.

Modern fantasy has its roots in fairy tales, myths and legends – an imaginary past, more than a real one. It is therefore less concerned with novelty and innovation, and more with old stories, retold. The very word 'novel' means 'new' – unlike the old, tried-and-tested, epic tale. Even the most inventive and original fantasy tends to look back to an earlier epic tradition, or to what might be considered eternal truths.

Archetypes, defined by my dictionary as the 'original pattern or model', are vital to fantasy. Examples of archetypes include the wise old woman, the witch, the divine child, the young hero (or heroine) sent on a quest, helpful animals, a walled castle, the wasteland, the dying king, shape-shifting tricksters, dragons, unicorns ... Landscape and plot elements, as well as characters, may be archetypal. If you read much fantasy you can probably make your own list of recurring character types and images and themes. When they're handled well, these familiar characters have the ring of truth about them, and seem both familiar and yet original; but if the author is lazy or unskilled, they'll come across as cartoons or clichés.

Theory

If you're interested in knowing more about the structure underlying fantasy tales, there are a number of good books on the subject: Joseph Campbell's *Hero With a Thousand Faces* or his four-volume study of religion, *The Masks of God*; Erich Fromm's *The Forgotten Language*; or Marina Warner's *From the Beast to the Blonde*. But beware: fascinating though it is, theoretical analysis of fantasy *won't* help you write it. Scholars and critics can unpick stories into their archetypal pieces, but the resulting diagram, no matter how clear, is not a useful blueprint for a writer.

Memorable fantasies are not composed by selecting three archetypes from Column A and two from Column B. It may be interesting to look at a work of fiction and pick out the archetypal characters and the classic pattern ('It's the hero's journey to enlightenment!') lying underneath, but I think that's something that should come afterwards, and preferably from the readers. The writer should concentrate on creating believable characters in an interesting story. You have to start from the personal – write about what deeply matters to *you*, write what you feel to be true, not what you think you 'should' say – and, with luck and skill, others will respond to it.

Updating the past

Another thing to bear in mind when thinking about 'classic' or traditional stories is the diversity and sophistication of the modern audience. Our popular culture is not passed on by word of mouth, as in the past. Characters like Sleeping Beauty or Little Red Riding Hood which originated in stories told and retold are now better known as Disney cartoons, as parodies, or as images in television advertisements. It's no longer enough simply to tell the same old stories in the same old way – and certainly not if you want to appeal to more than a very limited readership.

The bottom line of all genre fiction – not just fantasy – is the repetition of a few basic conventions in a limited range of variations. This very predictability is what makes it 'work' and appeal to a certain audience – but it is also what limits it as a literary form. Some people are drawn to genre fantasy, just as others are drawn to genre romance, as an escape from reality. They seek comfort in familiarity; they know the formula they like, they don't want to be disturbed or surprised, and some writers are obviously on the same wavelength and able to churn it out. However, this sort of formulaic fantasy will appeal only to the narrowest and least demanding readership, and in today's shrinking market will be hard to sell. To be successful, genre fantasy should be familiar enough to satisfy expectations, yet different enough to be surprising and distinctive.

Fantasy can also be subversive. And the best fantasies can reach levels and explore subjects inaccessible to other types of fiction.

Reality in fantasy

Even the most hard-headed, logical realist has dreams and fears. We all have fantasies, and because they are part of our personalities, they are important. We don't live on just one level, in the material world.

The general assumption is that our fantasy lives are less important, 'less real', than what is perceived to be our real lives. Children are allowed to pretend, but adults are only supposed to have one self, one personality, one linear life. Lovers may – riskily – share their sexual fantasies with each other; people in therapy are encouraged to talk about their inner lives; role-playing games and amateur dramatics are just about tolerated. But otherwise we're encouraged if not to repress them, then at least to keep quiet about our fantasies.

It can be nearly impossible to write about the imaginary, interior life in realistic fiction in a compelling, comprehensible way. But fantasy is ideal for this. It can heighten and intensify emotion, dramatise psychological states and put them centre stage. In a realistic novel, a storm may be a metaphor for the stormy relationship between hero and heroine, or it may be the setting to provide an exciting climax – the author may be using it to heighten emotion, while at the same time expecting readers to know that it's only weather. If the storm makes it harder for the lovers to reach each other, that's only chance (or poetic licence), and the sort of coincidence that might happen to anyone in the real world. In fantasy, though, even the weather may be meaningful; no background of shared reality can be taken for granted. A wizard may stir up a storm by magic, to foil his enemies. Or storms may foretell the coming of dragons, or be a battle between sky-lords.

Fantasies may have allegorical and metaphorical elements, but these aren't the whole story. It's not as simple as that. Stories about a young man or young woman learning how to use magic may be interpreted as being about growing up, and partly they are – but in that case, what does the magic stand for, in real life? Magic is a form of power, different from ordinary, earthly power. The best fantasies can't be translated into ordinary, realist terms. They have to work on their own terms.

Some fantasy is directly *about* fantasy. It may explore the consequences of desire – as in the fairy tales about people granted three wishes or, more grimly, W. W. Jacobs' 'The Monkey's Paw' about a mother who wishes her son back from the grave.

In *Mythago Wood*, Robert Holdstock invented a fragment of primordial woodland in southern England inhabited by mythagos, which he described as 'heroic legendary characters from our inherited unconscious'. These shape-shifting creatures express the desires, needs and fears of changing human culture down the centuries. Much of Robert Holdstock's work pursues his fascination with myth-creation, the origins of stories and language.

Alan Garner is another English fantasist who has written about the impact of mythic patterns on contemporary lives. In *The Owl Service*, three young people find themselves pulled into reliving the story of the Welsh hero Llew Llaw Gyffes, Blodeuwedd, the wife made for him by a wizard out of flowers, and Gronw, Blodeuwedd's lover and Llew Llaw's murderer.

Because fantasy isn't required to stick to the laws of the real world, it might be thought that anything goes. A story without limits would be as chaotic and mysterious as dreams, closer to surrealism than what most people expect when reading fantasy. Magic has rules – they're just not the same as the rules of logic. One of the great freedoms of fantasy is that you can make up your own rules. Once you've decided what they are, play fair: don't keep changing them, or ignoring them, or your readers will soon lose faith in you.

Emotional truth is vital when you're writing fantasy. Everything else is up for grabs, but your characters, and their feelings, must ring true. If they're believable, readers will accept their world, no matter how strange, and follow them through all sorts of bizarre adventures.

The science in science fiction

How much science do you need to know to write science fiction?

How long is a piece of string? It's up to you. Curiously, when people learn that I write SF they often ask, 'Do you know a lot about science?', but when they learn that I also write children's books they never say, 'Do you know a lot about children?'

Some scientists do write SF – Greg Benford, for example, is a physicist, and Paul McAuley is a biologist. Maureen McHugh is an anthropologist, Vonda McIntyre trained as a geneticist. Brian Stableford has degrees in biology and sociology, and Sir Fred Hoyle was an astronomer. If you have a particular field of expertise, whether it be particle physics, anthropology, marine biology or child psychology, using your knowledge can bring added depth and believability to your fiction.

However, the audience for particularly technical problem pieces – stories which exist to explore some scientific puzzle – is a small one. Those in the know will appreciate it when your scientific argument makes sense (and complain bitterly if it doesn't), but even scientists read fiction for entertainment, not instruction. Novels which are thinly disguised essays are rarely popular. What's important is the human meaning of the science – how does it affect the characters? And why should the reader care?

There are plenty of good, popular science books around to help you with your research if you know that a scientific back-ground is necessary for the story you want to tell. They're written for a general audience, so you don't need special training to understand them.

My own scientific training is nil. I could never get on with maths at school, which inhibited me from taking science courses at university. I was tempted by anthropology, but the require-ment of a course in statistics put me off. Even in science fiction, which I started reading as a pre-teenager, my preference was always for the more poetic, humanist writers like Ray Bradbury and Theodore Sturgeon than for the 'hard science' stories published in *Analog*. The fact that Ray Bradbury's vision of Mars is known to be impossible doesn't make *The Martian Chronicles* any less wonderful. It's still a classic of imaginative, visionary literature.

Much SF has little or no actual science in it, even when it takes a generally scientific attitude towards the world and avoids outright fantasy. Just as it is not necessary to know in detail how computers (or cars) work in order to write a story set in the contemporary world with characters driving cars to their work as computer programmers, so you can generally avoid explaining how the technology of the future works. If your characters are ordinary people rather than scientists, they may not understand it themselves; even if they are technicians, they are unlikely to stand around explaining it to each other! Although technically 'hard' SF shouldn't contain anything that contemporary science believes impossible, it often does. Faster-than-light travel is supposed to be impossible, but a vast chunk of SF would be impossible without it.

Your own tastes, interests, strengths and weaknesses as a writer will help you decide how much or how little real scientific content there is in what you write. There's room for all sorts.

Getting started

Some writers seem to be endlessly inventive, bursting with ideas, trying new things all the time. Others work slowly, often returning to the same few subjects again and again. Neither approach is necessarily better than the other, but it can be frustrating if you *want* to write but feel you have nothing to write *about*.

I can certainly remember that when I was in my teens and early 20s I was full of the will to write, and had plenty of time and energy – but nothing to say! Like many other young writers, I didn't have the experience, either emotional or practical, to write a novel until I'd grown up a little.

Garry Kilworth, who writes in a variety of genres for both children and adults, began his career as a science fiction writer. He's the envy of many of his friends and fellow writers for his ability to keep coming up with great ideas. However, he is convinced that anyone can do the same, with practice. He likes to compare the imagination to a muscle: the imagination needs exercise; the more you use it, the stronger it will get. Once you're in the habit of having ideas, they'll come more readily.

Keep a notebook. I can't stress how helpful this is. You may think you don't get ideas, simply because they pass quickly through your mind and are forgotten. Writing them down will keep you from forgetting – it will also give them a form. It may be difficult at first, but soon they'll start to seem more like ideas and less like random thoughts. Don't feel that you have to develop every idea, or justify it – just jot down your thoughts and reactions to things. Whenever something grabs your attention, make a note of it. If you're sitting and waiting for someone, why not describe the place where you are waiting? Or write quick sketches of the people around you, trying to imagine who they are. You can make lists of made-up words, names for characters or imaginary places. Include quotations that strike you from books you're reading, newspaper clippings, snatches of overheard conversation. Misunderstandings are good: Harlan Ellison tells about the story that came from mis-hearing the line 'Oh, Jeffty's fine – he's always fine' as 'Jeffty's five – he's always five' and imagining a boy who never grew up, who was always five years old.

I have heard some people say that a notebook is useless for them; they simply can't write 'on the run' like that. If the alternative of keeping a small tape-recorder at hand to speak into doesn't work, either, you might try the diary routine instead. Make it a habit to sit down with your journal once a day, whenever you can carve out 20 minutes for yourself, and jot down some of your impressions and thoughts from the previous 24 hours.

Read. Read a lot, and read widely. Not just fantasy, but all sorts of novels, and non-fiction too. Pursue any areas of interest – learning a lot about any subject may prove useful. Non-fiction is great for intriguing snippets which may grow into ideas. Read a newspaper. In magazines, I find *New Scientist* and *The Fortean Times* particularly full of potential story ideas.

Write. This is the most important thing that a writer does. Write every day, and always have a work in progress. Maybe you're waiting for the big idea, something fantastically original, something with bestseller potential, a real classic. While there's no harm in aiming high, you'll never get anywhere if you insist that everything must be perfect before you begin. If you're not ready to start a novel, and none of your ideas seem 'original' enough for a short story, allow yourself to write purely as an exercise, about whatever comes to hand. Try taking an incident from history and setting it in the far future, or rewriting a favourite legend or fairy tale in your own style. Write a reaction to something you've read – perhaps something you disagreed with, a story you found unbelievable, or characters you wanted to shout at or advise. If you enjoy poetry, why not 'translate' a favourite poem into a story in prose? Pick a couple of favourite symbolic objects (a cloak of invisibility, a magic wand, a key) and write about what might happen if such an object were to come into the possession of a ordinary person in the real world. Be playful and don't worry about criticism or the marketplace. This is just to get you limbered up.

You might try keeping a dream journal, writing what you can remember as soon as you wake up. I generally find that dreams are too bizarre, personal and chaotic to be turned into fiction, but some people find them a useful source, and it can help give you access to your own subconscious.

Be aware of your own responses, and be curious about other people and the world around you. When something catches your attention in a particular way, when a word or a phrase haunts you, when you puzzle over a particular incident in your life, keep returning to the same 'what if ...'. These are all clues that here is something you may need to write about.

Finally, remember Henry James' helpful advice to a young writer: 'Be someone on whom nothing is lost.'

The unimportance of ideas

In SF, especially, there is a tendency to over-stress the importance of 'ideas'. Inexperienced writers, and those who haven't read a lot of fiction, sometimes imagine that a 'brilliant idea' will make up for any weaknesses in style or plot. The reason that science fiction had such a bad name for so long (and still does, in some quarters) is that literary standards were so low in pulp magazines, where SF and fantasy first developed as a genre. Fans read SF stories for the ideas and the 'sense of wonder' – and tactfully ignored the unlikely characters and wooden dialogue.

But the pulp magazines and their low standards are gone. SF and fantasy have to compete on the same level as all other fiction in a more demanding market. 'Brilliant ideas' won't sell a book on their own.

Having the idea is only the beginning. Now it's time for the hard work.

3
World-Building

Landscape, in both SF and fantasy, is more than just background: it plays a role equivalent to that of a major character. The setting may determine the plot, or have been determined by it – either way, it is firmly bound up with the SF or fantasy story.

This is perhaps the major way in which fantasy and SF differ from other genres. In a romance or a mystery, the sense of place may be important, with local colour appreciated by the reader, but it is seldom vital to an understanding of the story. There are exceptions, of course. Diane Johnston's *Le Divorce* and *Le Marriage*, like many of Henry James' novels, are about the specific cultural conflicts encountered by Americans in France, and the stories hinge on that relationship. But most contemporary fiction is easily translatable from Paris to New York, London to Chicago, Chicago to Toronto – as of course often happens when a French or an English novel is brought to the screen by Hollywood. The story and characters remain the same; the setting is treated like wallpaper which can be changed to suit the audience.

This is impossible in SF and fantasy, where the imaginary world is more than just a setting for a story. Discovering and describing your background is as essential as the plot – usually, world-building is an inextricable part of the story, and the two tasks will go hand-in-hand. Often, creating your world begins to create the plot, and vice versa.

Readers *expect* that the world of the story will be different from the world that they live in; experienced SF and fantasy readers know they can't take anything for granted, and rely on the writer to tell them what they need to know to make sense of the story.

You can't rely on common knowledge to fill in the blanks, as the writer of contemporary realist fiction can – although there are some shortcuts which writers working in particular traditions may use (*see* 'SF and the Default Setting', pp. 46–48). For the most part, constructing a detailed, believable world is the major task of the SF and fantasy writer. How you go about it will depend a lot on your particular interests and aims in any given work.

Extrapolation

To extrapolate is to infer or conjecture beyond the limits of what is known, based on what *is* known. Extrapolation is a major tool of the SF writer. It's not the same thing as prediction, because SF writers don't expect their imaginary futures to come true. However, it does have to seem possible. The writer needs to convince the reader that this imaginary future is realistic, at least for the duration of the story. Market analysts and futurologists try to extrapolate what is most likely to happen, projecting from current trends, but the SF writer looks for the most interesting, dramatic possibilities, which are not usually the most likely.

One way of extrapolating is to take one particular trend – say, the current advances in genetic engineering and the discussion about the development of 'designer babies' – and to follow it to any logical extreme. If you assume that the government will strictly regulate reproduction, one type of future will suggest itself; if you think that market forces will prevail, another. What might be the short- and long-term impact on society? Different storylines are suggested by taking a different approach. You might assume that human cloning is just around the corner (on the day that I first drafted a version of this chapter, three years ago, scientists on the radio were solemnly predicting the first cloned human baby within two years) – or you might want to take the view that the many problems involved in animal cloning (numerous birth defects and still-births, vastly increased foetal size and weight, etc.) will make successful human cloning extremely rare. Will old-fashioned sexual reproduction go out of style? What sort of new problems might be caused by genetic engineering? Maybe things we now consider to be 'flaws' will be missed in a 'perfect' future. When beautiful is the standard, being ugly could be chic.

Another way of extrapolating is to work backwards. Start with the situation you want to write about – say, a world in which children are rare – and then figure out what sort of events might lead to such a situation. Some sort of plague? Widespread infertility as a side-effect of something else? Physical immortality?

You can also extrapolate backwards to create an alternative present-day world by imagining a major change in history as we know it. In Philip K. Dick's *The Man in the High Castle*, Japan and Germany divided America between them after winning the second world war. In Keith Roberts' *Pavanne*, the Protestant Reformation was crushed by the Catholic Church, and the Spanish Armada defeated England. In *The Years of Rice and Salt*, Kim Stanley Robinson asked how the world would look if the Black Death had wiped out European civilisation in the 14th century. The possibilities are endless.

Imaginary worlds

Perhaps you want to forget about our world, our possible futures, and write about something completely different. You might like the idea of an intelligent, civilised race evolved from dinosaurs, or from birds, and try to figure out what sort of cultures such a race would create. Or maybe your characters dwell among the stars, or beneath an ocean, or are gas-breathing giants in another world. It's entirely up to you.

You don't *have* to explain how or why the world you write about has come to be, and it doesn't have to be linked causally with our own world. Generally, in SF, some sort of linkage to our world is presumed, and may be sketched in or spelled out. However, in fantasy – and in a lot of space opera and far-future science fiction – writers don't bother. The secondary world is simply there, and needs no special justification.

When George R. R. Martin and I wrote *Windhaven*, we provided an explanatory science-fictional background. The story was set in the future, after humanity had moved out to colonise the stars. Windhaven was an uninhabited planet on which they crash-landed. It became, effectively, a 'lost colony', cut off from the rest of the universe and plunged back into a pre-technological existence by the crash of their spaceship and by the lack of available metal. The characters, therefore, are human – but with no memory of earth. Their histories and their society are entirely of Windhaven.

Perdido Street Station by China Mieville is set in another world – but unlike many fantasy worlds, which tend to be simpler and less technological than our own, this is a very urban, modern-feeling world. It contains both human and intelligent, non-human creatures co-existing on the same planet – although the reason for this bizarre mix of species is not given. Science, magic, technology and art all rub and jostle together in an urban setting. Mieville gives no more explanation for his bizarre setting than Mervyn Peake did for *Gormenghast* – it simply *is*, and is described in such vivid, realistic detail that the reader has to accept it, and even live in it, for the duration of the book.

You don't have to explain how your scenario came to exist, as long as you make it believable in context. The expression 'willing suspension of disbelief' is often used to describe how readers approach works of fantasy. They know that the story is not real, but agree to accept the fiction. Not to believe it, but to refrain from disbelieving. Suspending disbelief ... I think of it as a sword hanging on a thread above the page. You don't have to trick or browbeat or argue the willing reader into believing that what you say is true; all you need to do is give them a story and characters and a world they can enjoy, and they'll go along with you.

Consequences

Go ahead, be bold, present your world and don't worry about explaining how it came to be. But remember that events have consequences. Even in an imaginary world, actions ripple out and have an impact on everything else. When you're world-building, you need to consider the whole ecology, not just isolated details.

Political, economic and religious structures don't spring fully formed out of nowhere, nor do they usually continue unchanged for millennia. You don't have to work out a time-line of a thousand years of imaginary history – unless you want to! But you should realise that one thing leads to another ... and that some connections are more logical and likely than others. A society dominated by a powerful Christian church is unlikely to be sexually libertarian (unless Christianity developed along very different lines); hereditary kingship implies an entire hereditary class system; desert-dwellers have completely different customs and attitudes from people who live in a rain-forest. They'll have different attitudes towards water, property, the best way to live ... and their gods and belief systems will be different. Think of how geography and weather, as well as religion and economics, have affected people on earth throughout history, and bring that awareness to your fiction. Figuring out one aspect of your society may suggest all sorts of interesting story possibilities, as well as paving the way to understanding how other aspects might function. Consider how family arrangements are constructed. How are the children brought up and educated? Do women and men have equal rights? How is power conferred and exercised? Is your imaginary society divided along class-lines, by race, by age? The more you know about your fictional world, the richer and more believable it will seem to your readers.

Because you're not writing an essay, but fiction, most of the background information won't be presented in chunks of information but rather filtered throughout the story in the way in which characters react and how they live their daily lives. You need to be so well-informed about your world that you can describe it from the inside out, and avoid the kind of false notes or anachronisms that will jar the reader back into this world.

Here's an example I remember from a workshop many years ago. The story was set in an overcrowded, polluted near-future. The main character came back to her tiny apartment from work, had a meagre meal of tofu and rice, and took a bath. She lay there soaking, mourning lost comforts as she thought about food shortages, power outages, etc. Someone else in the workshop pointed out that given this background, soaking in a hot bath was an improbable luxury. It would be more likely – and make the future seem more real – for her to wash herself in a few inches of tepid water, which her husband would then use for his bath, following which the water would be carefully stored or put through a purifier for reuse ...

Such a little thing: a character having a bath. But that's exactly the kind of detail you need to remember when you're building your world. As you think about the major changes – who has power, how it is exercised, what the climate is like, etc. – don't lose sight of the little, everyday details. What do your characters eat? Where does the food come from? How do they cook it? If water is rationed, will they have some other way of keeping clean? What impact will this have on social relationships? On the spread of disease?

Research

If you are writing SF set in the near future, or trying to extrapolate believable advances in current technology, you must research your subject. In fantasy, a good deal can be made up (as long as it *feels* right), but if you want to write hard SF then research is essential. SF readers expect that scientific extrapolation should not contradict or ignore the known facts. And if you're writing about the known universe, whether it's the surface of the moon or the inside of a research laboratory, it's as important to get the details right, and to make them convincing, as it would be if you were writing a story set in contemporary Tokyo or New York. Greg Benford's *The Martian Race* is a near-future adventure story which attempts to demonstrate a plausible scenario for the exploration of Mars. The author's acknowledgements run to a page and a half of thanks to various experts for their help and advice.

When Brian Aldiss embarked on his *Helliconia* series, he sought expert scientific help in working out the physics and biology of his imaginary planet, whose primary sun is in an eccentric orbit around another star, thus giving Helliconia two sets of seasons – one of them a 'Great Year' over the course of which whole civilisations rise and fall.

An unknown writer would have a hard time getting busy and respected scientists from a variety of fields to offer suggestions or to 'explain puzzling details', as the well-known Aldiss and Benford could. Fortunately, though, there are books, magazines and websites to help you out. If you're starting from scratch in a particular field, you could do worse than read books written for children on the subject. They're written simply and accessibly and don't assume any prior knowledge. Once you have a clear idea of the basics, you can tackle more complicated material.

Talking to people who are 'in the know' can be useful, even when you're not embarking on an ambitious world-building exercise. They don't have to be famous. Research is helpful not only for world-building, but also for making your characters more varied and believable. If you're going to write about scientists, for example, you should have some idea of how they think, and what they do in their daily working lives. When I wanted to write about a mathematician for *Lost Futures*, I spent a couple of hours talking about the subject with a maths teacher. He was at great pains to stress that he was not a 'real' mathematician – but hearing his explanation of how he had come to that realisation, and his description of what 'real' mathematicians did, helped me very much in imagining my character.

Pseudo-science

When you're dealing with facts, you *must* get them right – unless you're deliberately changing them to signal to the reader that this is an alternative reality. This applies to fantasy as well as to SF, although no one can argue that 'magic doesn't work like that' if it's your own world, so to a large extent you can make your own rules in fantasy. But if you're going to start playing about with known reality, getting physical or historical facts wrong, you should have a reason for it – and you must be consistent. It's all right to set your story in a world in which people have gills as well as lungs, or Queen Victoria died at the age of 30, but there's a big difference between someone who changes the facts on purpose, and someone who simply gets them wrong. Readers *will* notice.

Arthur C. Clarke once said that descriptions of any sufficiently advanced technology are indistinguishable from magic, and that's a good point. Readers will expect to recognise the background of fiction set in the present, or a decade or so in the future, but far-future scenarios are likely to be very, very different. Writers of space opera can get away with justifying just about anything if they have a good line in pseudo-scientific patter: matter-transmitters; 'warp-drives' for interstellar travel; soul-keepers that store the human personality or download it into a newly cloned body ... it's all magic presented as futuristic science.

There are different ways of handling made-up science, and no hard-and-fast rules. What's plausible in one year sounds ridiculously old-fashioned in another. Standards change, along with other fashions. If you keep up with the latest trends reported in the press and also pay attention to what your fellow SF writers are doing, you'll know whether black holes or 'wormholes', chaos theory or instantaneous matter transmission via quantum mechanics is the currently popular wheeze for interstellar travel, and you should be able to avoid sounding silly. But some research is necessary to write almost any good, speculative fiction.

Don't ignore the facts

Inventing technology to achieve things that are currently impossible is OK. Meddling with facts is not. Don't try making up explanations for things for which there's already a solid working theory, or faking 'obscure' details, thinking that no one will notice. Some readers may be fooled, but those who notice that you got your facts wrong are likely to lose faith in your fiction as well.

The assumption that 'no one will notice' implies contempt for the audience, which is something no good writer should have. Many years ago a friend of mine was writing scripts for a short-lived SF series on American TV. In one script, the hero was stuck down a pit, and the producer wanted a 'more visual' and dramatic means of escape. He suggested that the hero use his laser-gun, bouncing the rays off the reflective sides of the pit to create a 'ladder' of laser-beams which he could climb up to escape ...

The writer stared at the producer in disbelief. 'But that's impossible. A laser is just a beam of light – even if it looked like a rung, there's nothing there!'

The producer shrugged impatiently. 'Nobody's gonna know that! Anyway, who cares? It'll look great!'

Special effects may mean the death of logic, or even common sense, as narrative is lost in spectacle. Film-makers assume – and they may be right – that people will put up with any amount of nonsense for the pleasure of watching a planet blow up. However, I suspect that the major loss of sense happens *after* the script has been written, when the writer's logical connections are cut in order to save screen time (explanations are 'boring') or to give more scope to the special effects. Remember that on the page, the special effects happen in the reader's head, produced by the words of the writer. If those words communicate the wrong images, or if they don't make sense, only the writer is to blame. Always assume that readers *will* notice if you get something wrong. After all, *you* would notice – wouldn't you?

As I've said before, you don't have to be a scientist to write science fiction. But you must be reasonably intelligent, able to think logically, and willing to grant your readership the courtesy of assuming the same about them.

Quantum theory as a plot device

When I started work on my novel *Lost Futures*, it was to explore a personal obsession with the idea of alternative realities. I wanted to write about someone who becomes aware of some of the other lives she might have lived, if she had made a different decision at a key moment in her past. I had already written about this in a short story, 'No Regrets,' using the idea of a house which is haunted by a child this woman never had. For the novel, though, I wanted to explore the idea in greater depth, and more theoretically. So I read as much as I could about the 'many worlds' theory underlying quantum mechanics.

I soon realised that this theory did not allow my initial notion – that my character could move back and forth between worlds. At first I felt frustrated, blocked by the impossibility; but gradually, when I realised that there was no way around it, I found myself having to move in another direction – and this turned out to be even more interesting than my first idea. I was still nervous that maybe I'd got it all wrong, so I was thrilled when *Lost Futures* was favourably reviewed in *The New Scientist*, as 'genuine SF' with 'sound scientific speculation at the heart of the story'. Research does pay off!

How closely you want facts to dictate your fiction, and how much research you need or want to do, is something only you can decide. Fantasy and SF are no different from other types of fiction in this respect. If you're writing about something you know, whether from personal experience or from reading, you'll be able to bring more conviction to the writing. If you avoid writing about things you don't already understand, you'll limit yourself unnecessarily. Don't be afraid of research. Even if it begins as a necessary chore, it will give you more ideas, and may lead you in unexpectedly exciting directions.

The need for factual details isn't limited to SF. Fantasy, too, needs to be anchored in specific, realistic detail. Many of these details may come out of your own experience. There is also more scope for the fantasy writer to simply make things up. But even the most fanciful of fantasy worlds must have some things in common with our reality in order to be comprehensible, and few writers have lives rich and varied enough to be able to call on their own experience all the time.

The Waldrop method

Some writers love researching – possibly even more than the writing itself. David Wingrove immersed himself in the history and culture of China before beginning to write his enormous *Chung Kuo* sequence about an alternative future world dominated by Imperial China. (A first-hand trip to China came only after he was well into it.) Although Dune was an invented world, Frank Herbert's *Dune* books obviously owe quite a bit to his understanding of Arabic desert societies. Mary Gentle has pursued her interest in warfare and fighting techniques not only far enough to write wholly convincing fiction, but also to the level of academic degrees.

And then there's Howard Waldrop, who spends far more time researching than he does writing. When he gets an idea, it is the beginning of a long process and many days in the library. For one short story, '... the World, as we Know't', Waldrop says: 'I spent six months researching everything, and I mean everything, about the subject, about 18th century physics and chemistry, Joseph Priestley, Lavoisier, the whole taco as they used to say ... About six months after I sold this, I found a copy of a doctoral dissertation written in the 1930s that had pulled together *all* of the research I'd done in three dozen books. Oh well, live and learn to use the subject index, I always say.'

In *Night of the Cooters*, Waldrop includes a story called 'Thirty Minutes Over Broadway', written for George R. R. Martin's shared-world anthology *Wild Cards*, along with ten pages of notes on the source material. Waldrop writes: 'People have always accused me of researching too much. It was three years between initial conception and the writing of this one ... The research was to lend what we in the rip-roaring days of Postmodernist Fiction used to call *verisimilitude*, but what is now referred to as "... making it seem real-like". I figure if I'm going to work this damn hard I might as well get some use out of it and some credit for it. Whether this adds to your enjoyment of the story, or only clutters up your mind as much as mine, I don't care.'*

SF and the default setting

World-building is hard work. It can be fascinating and fun, and the successful world-builder may feel a sense of godlike power after creating a logical and possible new world. But even if you enjoy the challenge, as many SF writers do, you don't necessarily want to construct an entire new world from scratch every time you get a good idea for a new story.

And it's not necessary. A lot of very good and popular SF has been published in which the background, while being necessarily different from our world, is not absolutely original. If you choose to use a standard SF setting, you'll need to customise it, but world-building becomes less a thing you have to work on and more a result generated by your story-line and characters. There's no need to explain how everything works if you provide enough convincing details. Here are some standard SF settings:

Very near future
Basically, this is our world ... only five, ten or 20 years from now. This type of SF may well be published as mainstream, and may postulate a taken-for-granted contemporary background with only a few technological improvements highlighted for plot reasons.

After the catastrophe
One satisfying way of dealing with troublesome complexity is to wipe it out via some huge natural disaster (the seas rising as a result of global warming is popular right now), worldwide

*Waldrop, *Night of the Cooters: More Neat Stories*

economic collapse combined with plague, alien invasion or (rather old-fashioned) nuclear war. Your story may deal with a few survivors struggling to rebuild civilisation in the wasteland, or take place decades or even centuries later, in whatever kind of social or political set-up you like.

Very far future, space opera

If human-kind makes it through the next few millennia, perhaps moving out to the stars, who knows what we'll be like? Your guess is as good as mine. The very far future can't be researched, only imagined. This sort of SF is closest to fantasy, despite its technological trappings, and may even be referred to as 'space fantasy' or 'science fantasy'.

Earth-like worlds

These may be exaggerations of one particular area on earth: an ice-covered planet, a desert world, a single futuristic city occupied either by an alien race or by human colonists. The worlds may have their own species, or be colonised by humans. You can invent whatever you like to suit your story. For the planet of Windhaven, George R. R. Martin and I imagined an ocean-world scattered with islands. We wanted to write about a caste of flyers, who maintain communication between the islands by riding the winds on metal wings, so we postulated slightly lighter gravity than that of earth, as well as more reliable winds, to make flying easier. In order to keep our characters in the low-tech setting which appealed to us, and to justify the scarcity of wings, we made Windhaven a metal-poor world. Farming and fishing are important industries. The plants and animals are similar to those found on earth.

Enclosed habitat

These may be spaceships or space-stations or cities under the sea or in hostile environments (post-nuclear holocaust or alien planet). They provide a limited, basic, standardised background as a setting for human drama. The atmosphere is that of the submarine, the office block, shopping centre, etc. which means that it is not hard to visualise or explain, being immediately recognisable by contemporary urban citizens.

Discovering your fantasy world

If SF writers are conscious of having to build their worlds, fantasy writers may more often feel that they have 'found' theirs. The landscapes of childhood often have a particularly strong impact. They turn up again and again in dreams and in books – although no one but the writer/dreamer may recognise their origin. A small hill may have seemed like a mountain to the child, so it becomes a mountain again in fantasy. A patch of woodland in Kent where he grew up became Robert Holdstock's magical *Mythago Wood*, and Alan Garner set many of his books in the area around Alderley Edge which had been his family's home for generations.

In *The Lord of the Rings*, Tolkien was writing about a landscape known to him from birth – the English hills and valleys – and also deeply familiar to him from his studies in language, history, and northern mythology. His 'Middle Earth' has been a huge influence on other fantasy writers; even people who haven't read Tolkien may 'know' him at second-hand, reflected in later works. Tad Williams, for example, has said that much of his *Memory, Sorrow and Thorn* trilogy consists of a 'commentary' on Tolkien.

Fantasy worlds don't have to be *possible* in the way that science fictional worlds do. One definition of fantasy is that it is about things which *could not happen*. Fantasy writers are free to contradict nearly everything we know about 'reality', including the laws of physics. But that doesn't mean that anything goes. If it is to be understandable to anyone besides the author, the fantasy world must make some sort of sense. The workings of the fantasy world must have an internal consistency; it must have rules. These rules don't have to be spelled out, and it may take a while for the reader to understand them, but they should be there. However different it might be from our own world, a fantasy world should still feel like a real place: part of its appeal to readers (not to mention the author) is precisely to imagine themselves living there. They should be able to immerse themselves in it. Above all, the secondary world of fantasy must seem *liveable*. There are exceptions – the *Alice* books of Lewis Carroll, or Mark Danielewski's *House of Leaves*, for example, are both fantasies, but they don't provide the sort of escapism offered by genre fantasies. The other worlds they depict have more to do with nightmares than with 'world-building'. It is the very lack of any consistent rules that makes the constantly mutating house in *House of Leaves* so terrifying. It's not a nice place to visit, and you certainly couldn't live there.

Symbolism can easily be read into landscape features – dark woods, the endless sea, a wasteland, a path through the woods are archetypes just as much as the old wise woman, the helpful companion animal and the hero. Physical archetypes are often used – consciously or otherwise – in art and literature, but they are particularly at home in fantasy fiction. Because they are so immediately recognisable, there is something both comforting and deeply powerful in the best symbolic landscapes.

Among the most popular influences on the worlds of contemporary genre fantasy are Arthurian legends, Celtic mythology, and the European dark or middle ages. Excursions abroad don't seem to be as popular with the mass readership, although some writers have made inventive and original use of the history and legends of other cultures. For example, Garry Kilworth used Polynesian culture and myths in his trilogy, *The Navigator Kings*, and Barry Hughart has written a series of Oriental fantasies. Go where your heart takes you, into your own dream-world.

Fantasyland

Familiar to anyone who has ever read any fairy tales or indulged in role-playing games like 'Dungeons and Dragons', Fantasyland is the default setting for fantasy. The author mentions things like castles and villages, wizards, elves, peasants, swords, horses, perhaps dragons, expecting readers to recognise the terrain and fill in the gaps for themselves. This is a very basic venue, usually heavily second-hand, for a story. It has affinities with the stock backgrounds of some other genres – the village and the country house of the 'cosy' British mystery; the frontier town of the western – and works in a similar way. The reader is instantly at home, and the writer doesn't have to work too hard at invention or description. Enjoyable stories may be set in Fantasyland, but the resulting books will never be the most memorable or best that fantasy has to offer. John Clute has called Fantasyland 'a particularly useful thought-free setting for authors of shared-world enterprises and extended series'.

For a sharp-eyed look at the clichés involved here, see Diana Wynne Jones' amusing *The Tough Guide to Fantasyland*.

Are maps necessary?

A map at the beginning of a novel is like a signpost proclaiming, 'Here Be Fantasy'. For Tolkien, maps were part of the whole apparatus – glossaries, appendices, histories, drawings – which grounded and linked his fantasy to his academic studies. After Tolkien, maps quickly became something that every secondary-world fantasy had to have. Many people enjoy them, and fantasy readers have come to expect them. I was told by one editor that 'the fans miss it if it's not there'.

If you like map-making, or if it helps you to plan your world, go ahead and draw a map for your own use. But it's probably wise *not* to include it when you send off your manuscript. *After* you've sold the book is the time to mention any maps or other additional, extra-textual material you've created; the publisher may wish to use it, or to hire a professional artist to provide a map for the frontispiece. But while the book is still unsold and in manuscript form, the inclusion of artwork, appendices, jacket designs and so on may be 'a major turn-off', according to agent Antony Harwood, who sees such things as an indicator that 'the writer is more interested in window-dressing than content'. I don't know how many other agents or editors feel the same way, but it's worth keeping in mind that you'll look more professional if you leave out those little home-made 'extras'.

Describing your world

Even if you've provided a map to inform your readers up front that this world consists of two continents – one with mountains in the north, the other with a vast desert in the south – and the names of all important settlements and major geographical features, you'll still have to bring it to life on the page.

Not everything has to be spelled out, certainly not right away. I often find, when I begin writing a book or a story, that I have a huge mass of information about my characters and the situation which it seems urgent to get across in order to begin the story. But, since wholesale instantaneous information-transfer from one brain to another simply isn't possible, some things do have to wait. Choices have to be made. The economy of the 'establishing shot' in a film isn't so easily available in print. However, the fact that the book has been published as fantasy, the cover and, yes, the map, all tell readers that this fictional world is not the same as the one they live in. They'll go along with you, eager to discover more yet happy to wait, gradually learning more about your world as the story unfolds.

Many fantasy stories take the form of a journey, so the reader is in the same position as the main characters – travelling through the land and discovering it, and revealing themselves at the same time. In others, characters from our world enter another reality, which they have to learn about. Examples of this include *The Chronicles of Thomas Covenant* by Stephen Donaldson, and *Mythago Wood* and *Lavondyss* by Robert Holdstock.

Although *The Lord of the Rings* comes equipped with a prologue offering a great deal of background ('Concerning Hobbits', 'Of the Ordering of the Shire', and so on) and ends with many appendices including calendars, chronologies, family trees and other scholarly apparatus implying that this is a true history, this is neither necessary nor advisable practice for most writers. It will certainly add to the richness of your fantasy world if you, the writer, know the history of it in detail, but that doesn't mean your novel has to come with footnotes and time-lines. If it helps you, then by all means create chronologies and character lists and whatever else you need. You can decide when you've finished writing whether any of this material should be included in an appendix, or whether it should be filed away with your notes and early drafts – or possibly (and increasingly popular these days), posted on a website.

Long, detailed 'scene-setting' was acceptable in a more leisurely age, but if you take two pages to describe the landscape every time the scene changes, your readers are likely to put the book down and turn on the TV. It's not desirable, and, in a short story, it's not even possible.

Take a look at the most popular fantasy novels published in the last ten years, even the very longest, and you'll see that background description is integrated with the action. What's important is telling the story. The reader learns more and more about the world, and about the characters, as the story progresses.

Writing about how she handled the setting for one of her very early stories, Joanna Russ confessed that when she wrote it she wasn't ready to create 'a whole, self-consistent fantasy world'. So, she explained, in writing the story she 'piloted round [her] own incapacity to imagine a whole world by one very simple and unconscious principle: *the setting is important only as it impinges upon the protagonist*'.*

This is similar to Willa Cather's reaction to the old-fashioned, heavily descriptive novel. Rather than give the sort of detailed descriptions of houses, rooms, furniture and clothing which padded out most popular novels of her day, Cather invented the 'unfurnished novel' for herself, and included descriptive detail only when it was vital to the story or could be used to reflect the characters' state of mind. Ernest Hemingway did much the same

*Wilson, *Those Who Can*

thing. Even though Cather and Hemingway were writing books set in worlds that their readers could be expected to recognise, the SF and fantasy writer can learn a lot from this approach by always giving descriptions a purpose, connecting them to character and plot.

Description is most effective when it is woven into the action, and best when it comes with an emotional charge by being filtered through a character's perceptions. If they are at home in the world, the characters will not spend a lot of time concentrating on the details which are ordinary and familiar to them. If, as in the case of the Joanna Russ story, the setting is the antagonist, the protagonist will probably be too busy struggling to stay alive to allow for protracted scene-setting. The writer can concentrate on the action, telling the reader only as much as they need to know to understand and visualise what's going on.

SF as a special case

People who love SF often read it for more than just a good story, or a temporary escape from the real world. They want to be made to think, in the same way that some people particularly enjoy the puzzle aspect of mysteries. The SF fan will put up with a sense of dislocation and bewilderment for longer than a reader of other genre fiction. To some extent, the sense of dislocation, of being a stranger in a strange land, is part of the appeal of SF.

Just as with fantasy, the structure of the SF story may be that of a journey of discovery. Sometimes an alien world will have the status of a character, and the relationship between the human characters and their surroundings is the main thrust of the story. Characters in a fantasy are often deeply embedded in their world from the start, whereas in SF the characters may perceive a world from the outside – literally, as they arrive from space. The setting of an SF novel may have been carefully contrived to suit the plot, or the world may come first and dictate the story. Your own interests and reasons for writing will determine your aim and treatment.

How much information does the reader need? Sometimes, surprisingly little. A few vivid details can go a long way. If the story is compelling enough, the reader will be satisfied with a fairly sketchy background. Think of writing as being something like an impressionistic painting: a few lines and splashes of colour can evoke a whole scene. Readers do a lot of the work themselves, and are capable of extrapolating from the clues you give them to fill in the missing pieces and rebuild your world inside their heads.

The telling detail

If you find yourself overwhelmed by the task of describing your imaginary world, keep it simple.

The more *you* know about your world, the better. But everything you know doesn't have to be set down on the page. Your understanding will inform what you write. Too many long, elaborate descriptions can get in the way: they can be confusing rather than enlightening. Yes, the background is particularly important in fantasy and SF. But it shouldn't distract from the story. The writer may have the big picture in mind, but the reader wants to follow the story, and will be interested only in the important details: what matters to the characters, how the background affects the story.

Small, telling details can be enormously effective in giving the impression of a different reality. A famous example is Robert Heinlein's 'casually dropped-in reference' to a door that 'dilated' as a character entered a room. Harlan Ellison recalled reading that for the first time: '[I] was two lines down before I realised what the image had been, what the words had called forth. A *dilating* door. It didn't open, it *irised*! Dear God, now I knew I was in a future world ...'*

*Delany, *The Jewel-Hinged Jaw*

Through the eyes of the characters

The best way into any imaginary world is via a sympathetic character. The reader is drawn in by the experiences of view-point characters, and learns about the world by sharing their perceptions. If you start with a viewpoint character who is at home in this world, you can refer to things around him or her in a matter-of-fact way, without elaborate explanations.

Consider the following:

> The sky above the port was the colour of television, tuned to a dead channel.
>
> 'It's not like I'm using,' Case heard someone say, as he shouldered his way through the crowd around the door of the Chat. 'It's like my body's developed this massive drug deficiency.' It was a Sprawl voice and a Sprawl joke. The Chatsubo was a bar for professional expatriates; you could drink there for a week and never hear two words in Japanese.
>
> Ratz was tending bar, his prosthetic arm jerking monotonously as he filled a tray of glasses with draft Kirin. He saw Case and smiled, his teeth a webwork of East European steel and brown decay. Case found a place at the bar, between the unlikely tan on one of Lonny Zone's whores and the crisp naval uniform of a tall African whose cheekbones were ridged with precise rows of tribal scars. 'Wage was in here early, with two joeboys,' Ratz said, shoving a draft across the bar with his good hand. 'Maybe some business with you, Case?'
>
> Case shrugged. The girl to his right giggled and nudged him.
>
> The bartender's smile widened. His ugliness was the stuff of legend. In an age of affordable beauty, there was something heraldic about his lack of it. The antique arm whined as he reached for another mug. It was a Russian military prosthesis, a seven-function force-feedback manipulator, cased in grubby pink plastic.

By the end of the first page of *Neuromancer* by William Gibson we know we're in some future time, in Japan or some Japanese colony, in a zone known as the Sprawl (the name suggests a vast urban area; if not one city, perhaps several which have spread into each other) which has a large population of multi-ethnic expatriates, professionally employed. The bar and its mixed clientele are readily familiar, suggesting that although there have been many changes and advances (beauty is 'affordable' even to a mutilated barkeeper), we're not *too* far from now (television and beer are still popular). This is Case's world, and although we don't know what his business is, or what 'joeboys' might be, the authority of the narrative suggests that if you read on and pay attention you'll pick it up. Even if you never understand everything about how this future world operates, you'll have the *feel* of it, which is all that really matters for understanding the story.

When you're writing, keep thinking about what your characters might notice – but also the things they *wouldn't* notice, because these things are invisibly familiar to them. Such details, presented calmly and without explanation, can be very effective in building a sense of fascinating *otherness* into your world.

Explanations

On the third page of William Gibson's *Neuromancer* we learn that Case is, literally, burnt-out. Two years earlier he'd been:

> '... a cowboy, a rustler, one of the best in the Sprawl. He'd been trained by the best, by McCoy Pauley and Bobby Quine, legends in the biz. He'd operated on an almost permanent adrenaline high, a byproduct of youth and efficiency, jacked into a custom cyberspace deck that projected his disembodied consciousness into the consensual hallucination that was the matrix. A thief, he'd worked for other, wealthier thieves, employers who provided the exotic software required to penetrate the

bright walls of corporate systems, opening windows into rich fields of data.

He'd made the classic mistake, the one he'd sworn he'd never make. He stole from his employers. He kept something for himself and tried to move it through a fence in Amsterdam. He still wasn't sure how he'd been discovered, not that it mattered now. He'd expected to die, then, but they only smiled. Of course he was welcome, they told him, welcome to the money. And he was going to need it. Because – still smiling – they were going to make sure he never worked again.

They damaged his nervous system with a wartime Russian mycotoxin.

Strapped to a bed in a Memphis hotel, his talent burning out micron by micron, he hallucinated for thirty hours.

The damage was minute, subtle, and utterly effective.

For Case, who'd lived for the bodiless exultation of cyberspace, it was the Fall. In the bars he'd frequented as a cowboy hotshot, the elite stance involved a certain relaxed contempt for the flesh. The body was meat. Case fell into the prison of his own flesh.'

This is what is known in Hollywood as 'backstory' – it's the stuff that has happened before the story begins. Athough writers are often (rightly) exhorted to 'show, don't tell', a summary 'telling' may be more appropriate than lengthy flashbacks. It's efficient, not only in informing us about Case (who, we learn a few lines further on, has come to Japan in the hope – now exhausted along with his cash – of finding a cure for what has been done to him), but also for sketching in a little of his world.

Vivid, telling details are wonderful. They're often memorable. But they're not always the most effective way of getting across complex information. Sometimes explanations, delivered in simple, flat statements of fact, are required. Don't be afraid to spell things out when you have to.

4
Structuring and Developing Your Story

Like most genre fiction, SF and fantasy are largely *plot-driven*. This means that the plot, or story, is of major importance. That's not to say that character or style are any less important than plot, or that these three vital ingredients of fiction really exist independently of each other. Even calling them 'ingredients' is misleading, implying that 'plot' and 'characters' and 'style' are separate things like eggs or sugar which the authorial cook can add more of or forgetfully leave out altogether. In practice, plot, character and style are intertwined and co-dependent from the very beginning.

But for the purposes of this discussion, we can try to look at them separately. I'll talk about style in the next chapter. For now, let's consider plot and character.

Plotting

Critics and authors of literary fiction often disparage 'mere' story-telling – like Martin Amis, they emphasise their concern with language, and dismiss plot as a minor detail. I recently read an interview with the American writer Jayne Anne Phillips, in which she declared a lack of interest in narrative: 'I don't really believe in it,' she said. The same newspaper interviewed Irish novelist John Banville, who confessed, 'I've never been very good at plot' – his new novel was reviewed further down the page under the headline, 'With prose like this, who needs a plot?'

Yet most readers, critics to the contrary, pick up novels in the hope of being told a compelling, involving story. This is particularly true in genre fiction. No matter how well it is written, no matter how vivid the landscape, how sympathetic the characters, how unusual the basic idea – without a plot there *is* no novel. Even if what the readers remember afterwards is the fascinating premise, or the unusual aliens, or the strange and vivid other world, the writer's ability to construct a satisfying, workable story is what kept them reading.

From my own experience, I know that plotting can seem a daunting task. For years, as a short-story writer, I managed to evade the issue. In my earliest published stories there is little in the way of plot: they concern incidents; they are mood-pieces. Strange things happen, without explanation: a man falls in love with a mermaid; a little girl discovers that one of her dolls is cannibalistic; a woman finds out that her ordinary life is a drug-induced dream which enables her to survive in an horrific future society. The strangeness of the situation is the story. In 5,000 words or fewer there's no room for subplots or too many complications. I'm sure that many new writers feel, as I did, that plotting a whole novel is impossibly difficult.

It's true that some novels have enormously complicated plots, or a series of intertwined plots, full of elaborate twists and turns. And some quite simple plots are made to seem complex by the way in which the story is told, with revelations gradually doled out to the reader. But let's leave all these complications for later, and start with the basics.

Basic plots

Robert Heinlein once claimed there were only three basic plots: 'Boy meets Girl', 'The Little Tailor' and 'The Man Who Learned Better'. In response, Brian Stableford later pointed out that all three of Heinlein's plots could be seen as variants on a single 'Success Story' – success in love, in career, and in adapting to the ways of the world – and implied the possibility of the 'tragic variant' in which success was *not* achieved. Others have suggested that the number of 'basic plots' is seven, or ten, or 12, or 20. Or perhaps only one. John Gardner said that 'the basic – all but inescapable – plot form is: A central character wants something, goes after it despite opposition (perhaps including his or her own doubts), and so arrives at a win, lose, or draw'.* Whatever your feelings about this question, it can be a useful exercise to analyse the plots of a few popular novels, to see how far you can break them down, and what they have in common with each other.

All plots are about *something that happens to someone*. (In Heinlein's example, inevitably, the 'someones' were all men; but they could as easily be women, animals or aliens, so long as they are presented as conscious and potentially sympathetic beings.) In other words, plots feature one or more characters, and concern action over time. They have a beginning (introduction to the characters and situation), a middle (action; working out of conflict), and an end (resolution of conflict).

Conflict

Plots are fueled by conflict – it's hard to imagine a story without it. It may be a conflict between individuals (the main character, or *protagonist*, against another character, the *antagonist*); between an individual and society; between humans and nature (or some equivalent outside force); or it can be a psychological struggle actually within the protagonist. Whether on a grand scale (a war between two species for control of the universe) or at a very personal level (a woman deciding which of two men to marry), the conflict must come to a climax before a resolution is achieved.

A standard story pattern, or 'plot formula', which underlies a lot of popular fiction runs like this: A sympathetic main character has an urgent problem. Every effort to solve this problem makes the trouble worse. Eventually, the character figures out what must be done, having learned from what has gone before, and takes action – either succeeding in solving the problem, or failing tragically.

There are other story-patterns, such as the love story, the quest, the mystery, and the coming-of-age. All of these put one or more characters through various trials and experiences which

*Winokur, *Advice to Writers*

60

change them, and end – even when the pattern or journey is circular, returning to the starting point – with the original situation altered.

Plot formula versus situation

This may sound mechanical. It can be. When a plot is forced or imposed it usually rings false, at least to the sensitive reader. I suspect that's why writers who want to be seen as 'literary artists' profess to disdain plot. Many writers, in fact, do not consciously plot their novels – although that's not to say that the resulting book is plotless. In his memoir, *On Writing*, Stephen King says that his most plotted novels (*Insomnia*, *Rose Madder*) are 'stiff, trying-too-hard novels'; whereas a book like *Bag of Bones,* although it appears to be carefully plotted, actually grew out of a situation ('widowed writer in a haunted house') which allowed the details to arise 'spontaneously'.

If you begin with a situation that interests you and write about believable characters, some sort of plot will arise if you pay attention to their interaction. There must be some sort of conflict inherent in the situation, though – a devoted, loving couple living together in a utopian society won't give rise to much of a story unless you introduce trouble into their cosy paradise. You'll need to resolve the problem by the end, too, or you will alienate and infuriate your readers – although a partial resolution or ambiguous ending is a possibility.

Fiction without conflict or resolution isn't satisfying, however well it may be written. There is a human need for story. We look for patterns even where they don't exist: when life doesn't seem to make sense, we tell stories so that it does. Plot perceived at this level, as pattern, is the structural underpinning – a framework on which you can build your novel. Whether it is a tale of ambition, love, adventure, mystery or self-discovery doesn't matter. Even if there are only a few basic plots, they are endlessly flexible and your own originality will come through in the details – which are not insignificant, since they include absolutely everything that distinguishes one novel from another – of action, event, ideas, style and characters.

Complications

In a short story, you must keep your plot simple. In a novel, you can (indeed, must) add complications and delay your resolution. You may want to weave in other stories – known as *subplots* – by bringing in other viewpoint characters, or by having your main character fall in love or become involved in other activities and conflicts that have little or no direct bearing on the initial problem.

Some novels have very tightly woven, tightly focused plots: everything that happens tightens the screws of the main conflict, raises the stakes and puts the main character more at risk until the explosive climax. Others are more episodic, and may consist of a number of interwoven stories. In multi-volumed fantasies there is usually a big, continuing story which may take years, or many lifetimes, to work out; but there are also stories within the story – ideally, each book should have its own plot which will achieve climax and resolution, while adding to and advancing the overall plot of the series.

Over-plotting

It is possible to plot too much. Some writers put in so many startling twists and turns and complications into their novels that readers may get lost, or start to feel that they're only being asked to admire the author's cleverness, not allowed to become involved in a believable story. If this happens to you, try concentrating less on events and more on your characters. Are they believable and distinct? Have you made your main character too much of a superhero? You might want to consider cutting and simplifying the action, going for quality rather than quantity. Just because anything can happen in fantasy doesn't mean that absolutely everything should.

Finding your story

You must write about what matters to you. If you construct a story in a mechanical way, the artificiality will show. Plot *is* important. But it must be appropriate to your material and to your interests. You have to believe in it.

Look at your favourite books and stories. What draws you to them? For many people there is a myth or classic tale or character which has a particularly personal resonance. It might be 'Beauty and the Beast' or the story of Icarus; the little mermaid or the minotaur in the labyrinth. Classic story-lines are both universal and personal: a mother searches for her lost daughter; a poor, abandoned child grows up to discover that he's the heir to the throne; 'Psyche and Cupid' or 'King Lear' – such tales are always being reused and retold in different settings, with different characters. They can be set on other planets or in other lands, in the future or in the past.

Having the basic structure of a story will free you from worrying about plot, so you can concentrate on other details, like setting and psychology. Often in old stories, and particularly in myths, characters behave foolishly because they're *required* to do something by the demands of the story. The contemporary equivalent – for example, the character who goes back to the haunted house alone, after dark – raises howls of annoyance from modern readers, so you'd better do something about it. This doesn't have to mean changing the plot – instead, you may need to consider your characters more carefully, and give them a plausible motive for behaving in a way that seems foolish at first glance. On the other hand, you may find the traditional outcome unsatisfactory. If so, feel free to change the ending – or any other aspects you dislike. The princess doesn't have to marry the prince.

It's also worth remembering that the hero isn't the only one with a story to tell. Why not reimagine the story from the viewpoint of a minor character, or let the wicked witch tell her side of it? Even villains are heroes in their own minds, and may be able to justify every single nasty thing they do. Witches and vampires, once always the baddies, are now often the main characters in popular fiction. Marion Zimmer Bradley brought new life – and a new readership – to the Arthurian saga by refracting the subject through the lives of the women involved.

It's not only ancient material which is open to reinterpretation. Robert Louis Stevenson's *Dr Jekyll and Mr Hyde* was revisited by Valerie Martin in *Mary Reilly*, and by Emma Tennant in *Two Women of London: The Strange Case of Ms Jekyll and Mrs Hyde*.

The influence of J. D. Salinger's *The Catcher in the Rye* on Sylvia Plath's *The Bell-Jar* is not so obvious, but we know from Plath's journals that she consciously and deliberately modelled her autobiographical novel on Salinger's much-admired book; it gave her the structure that she wanted as a framework for her own story.

Gwyneth Jones has said that her basic story-lines are 'not infrequently ... filched from folklore, or some other kind of sacred text; or from the romantic fiction of a generation or two ago'. *Love On-Line*, my novel for young adults, sets Shakespeare's *Twelfth Night* in an American high school and in virtual reality. And, of course, Shakespeare borrowed plots wherever he found them.

Taking another book as your model for the pacing and placement of events is not plagiarism. Story-lines are flexible and as reusable as a clothes-line – but do take care that the clothes you hang on them aren't also borrowed!

Characters

Whose story is it?

In working out your plot, the first and most vital question you must answer is: whose story are you telling? That one decision will determine all that follows.

In the next chapter I'll go into more detail about viewpoint. For now, let's talk about character.

I can't really think about characters apart from story. To me, the two are inseparable aspects of the same thing. In the words of Henry James: 'What is character but the determination of incident? What is incident but the illustration of character?' I've heard some people talk about having ideas for characters and then looking for a story to 'use' them in, but this is alien to my experience. I've never in my life sat down to 'create a character' or had one pop up in my imagination, divorced from situation.

For me, a story or novel begins with an idea, often a situation with a character *implied* – the character develops as the story grows, and the two feed into each other. This may be a woman who finds herself remembering bits of lives she hasn't lived (*Lost Futures*), a man who digs up an alien parasite in his back garden ('The Colonisation of Edwin Beal'), the invention of a means of communicating with the dead ('Dead Television'), a future in which the well-off can opt for second childhoods ('The Poor Get Children'), or a boy who can turn himself into a big cat (*Panther in Argyll*).

Let's say you begin with only the most general idea of what you want to write about – commercialised production of human clones, or the struggle for leadership in an imaginary kingdom. Finding out *whose* story you want to tell will help you determine much about your plot. This is the single most important decision you can make, when beginning your work of fiction, because everyone has a different story. If you don't know whose story you want to tell – if you don't feel drawn instinctively towards a particular viewpoint – try asking yourself, *Whom does this hurt?* The answer to this question should give you a character with a dramatic problem, and a natural direction for plot development.

In the cloning story, your main character might be a boy who discovers that his 'parents' are really hired keepers; he's in fact the cloned property of a millionaire, the man's insurance against accidents. (This was the starting point for my short story 'Belonging'.) The story might be about how he comes to discover the truth about his life; or it might begin with his discovery: how can he escape his fate? Alternatively you might tell the story of a young woman hired to give birth to and raise a cloned child. She's come to love him as her own child; what will she do when ordered to hand him over for an organ-harvest? Or maybe the main character is a young man who will die without a heart transplant, but faces a moral dilemma when he finds out that the 'insurance policy' his parents bought for him is actually another young man, a living organ-bank. What will he do?

Once you start answering the questions you raise, you've begun to plot. If you create complex, believable characters, and are honest about what they might do, and the consequences of their actions, any more conscious plotting should be unnecessary. If you can trust your characters, they'll do it for you.

Plotting through character

My own SF novel, *Lost Futures*, was described in at least one review as a 'character study', and it is true that without the viewpoint character, Clare Beckett, the story would not exist: the novel is entirely about her life and character in a variety of incarnations.

Yet the novel did not begin with a particular character, but with an idea: what if someone could make contact through their dreams with other lives they might have lived under other circumstances, with their own alter egos? I wanted to write a small-scale, individual, intimate version of the alternate history idea based on the 'many worlds' theory. Instead of 'What if the Nazis had won?', I wanted to ask personal questions – the things that loom large not in history texts but in private lives.

I wanted my main character to be a woman of about my own age with something in her past which she was unable to stop regretting and leave behind. I knew nothing else about her, but before I could start writing I had to decide what her great regret was. At first I thought it would revolve around her decision not to have children, but for a woman in her 30s this would be a continuing decision, not a single deciding moment. I wanted her single, but I didn't want to write a whole book about an obsessive romantic who would waste her life pining after some guy who hadn't stuck around. Her regret had to be for something serious and irrevocable – a death, one she believed herself to be responsible for. A death she could have prevented.

Figuring out who had died, and how, told me more about Clare's family background and relationships. Gradually, as I wrote, she began to take on more reality, to become a real person rather than a vague notion.

Are characters necessary?

There is a hoary old argument within science fiction which holds that characters aren't really important to SF, and that attempts at creating old-fashioned, well-rounded characters such as you'd find in mainstream fiction are a waste of time because they distract attention from the *ideas* which are SF's entire reason for being. While it's true that some works of visionary SF, like Olaf Stapledon's *Last and First Men* or William Hope Hodgson's *The House on the Borderland*, deal with issues on a scale far removed from indvidual personalities, this argument is more often used as an excuse by writers who don't want to put in the hard work required to write convincing characters, preferring to use a few stock figures or character types (strong, handsome hero; brainy scientist; spunky female sidekick) to illustrate their stories.

The equivalent argument for fantasy is that fantasy uses archetypes and symbols to get at the truth; that realistic characters belong to realistic novels, not in the other-worlds of fantasy. It's certainly true that in myths and folktales, characters tend to represent one particular facet of the self, and are not complex, many-sided individuals. A psychoanalytic view of fairy tales has it that they dramatise internal or psychological struggles by splitting the self into component parts: the old witch, the foolish mother and the young maiden are all aspects of the same person, as are the hero, the villain, the fool and the helper.

But novels by their nature are about people. Modern fantasy novels aren't folktales or myths (although short stories may take those forms as models), and few SF novels are truly so metaphysically amazing that believable characters would be superfluous. Some authors, like Kafka and Borges, were never interested in depicting believable, realistic individuals, and wrote brilliant stories without them. But, although brilliant, Kafka and Borges are dangerous models for the novelist. The short story may be more accommodating to experiment. But the novel, by definition, has characters and a plot, and is judged by their quality.

Where do characters come from?

Ursula LeGuin writes about 'finding' her characters, and most writers would agree that there's no simple, obvious method to creating characters. My own experience is that I write the story, and the story writes the character. That's how it feels, anyway. The story could not exist without the characters, but the characters can't begin to exist before their story. Although I am conscious of 'making up' some things about them – deciding that a particular character will be tall and thin and lugubrious, for example, rather than plump and mysteriously sad – they then develop in ways that don't seem entirely under my control.

My advice, if you have a story but know nothing about the characters who populate it, is simply to start writing – even if you only have the beginning of a story; the opening situation. Start writing about the person in the situation. Don't worry about 'working up' characters beforehand with lists of their likes and dislikes, physical appearance, etc. If it's a story, it must have characters. Give them names. Names *are* important, yes, but sometimes you have to risk making a mistake. You're not chiselling them in stone, anyway, and if the names turn out to be all wrong, you can change them later. For now, if you're stuck, the important thing is to get them moving. Don't worry that this will take the story in the wrong direction – let it take *you*. This is research, this is a journey of discovery. You'll learn, as you go, how you'll have to change the characters (Someone with such a bad temper would *never* be in control of a starship! Surely a telepath would be more, er, empathic? Why on earth would she trust someone like *him*?) to make your story work – or you'll find yourself writing a different story to accommodate them.

I'm always a bit suspicious of the notion of characters who 'take over' a story, forcing the poor author to throw away their plans and watch helplessly as the characters act out their own plot. However, if that's how it seems to work for you, fine. At the other extreme is the author who considers the characters to be puppets of a pre-determined plot, and will not change it, no matter what. I would have thought that would *never* work, but Gwyneth Jones says that this is her method: 'I always know

68

what's going to happen, but the *why* develops ... Another way of looking at it: my synopsis marks out my playing field. This is the arbitrary grid which – because it *doesn't* always hang together – forces me to develop my characters into more "natural" complexity. I often find myself in an impasse – as who does not? – where it suddenly becomes obvious that such and such a sequence of events does not make sense: Why should she believe him when he tells her X ...? If he had the sense of a flatworm he wouldn't go through that door ... But she has to believe the unlikely tale, and he has to open the dreadful door, or my plot goes bust – *and I never change my plot for no one.* (Well, hardly ever). So off I go, looping around, inventing little curlicues of childhood trauma, quirks of obstinacy; whatever, to make the absurd into the necessary,' she wrote in 'Characters and How They Grow'.* 'I don't invent them as people. I invent them as a set of actions – a particular shaped space within the structure of the story: *the sulky hero, the wise courtesan.* Then I go round and round that space, like one of those little plastic spirograph things, in my redrafting, and gradually, magically, the reiteration of arbitrary-looking lines becomes a pattern: a pattern that feels to me like a person.'

Whether you believe that character or plot comes first, the important thing is that the two must fit together – seamlessly. Achieving the appearance of inevitability (Of course that character would behave like that! Of course that would happen next!) is *not* easy, but it's what you must accomplish.

Readers learn about characters by reading about them; writers, by writing. Some writers may feel that their characters have a real existence, but, practically speaking, characters are words on the page. That's all. Writing is a continuous series of choices: each choice that you make will partially determine future choices. Pay attention to the characters you are discovering. People *are* contradictory and multi-faceted, but we have expectations that people will stay 'in character' most of the time, in life – and even more so in fiction.

*Focus, Issue 24, June/July 1993

Characterisation in SF

One of the problems specific to SF is how to create believable future worlds or alien environments that seem convincingly different while still being comprehensible to contemporary readers. This problem is even more glaring when it comes to characters.

You can only write about what you know; for characters, you can draw on your experience of knowing and observing people in real life, and from your understanding of human nature. Fictional characters, like the people we meet, are revealed through their physical appearance, speech, interaction with others, habits, mannerisms, lifestyle and actions. In addition, in fiction we're also allowed to know what at least some of the characters are thinking and feeling.

Writers as different as A.S. Byatt and Stephen King can make us feel that we know characters intimately by simply showing them eating breakfast. Mentions of muesli, the *Guardian* and fresh coffee suggests one particular type of household; Pop-Tarts, burnt toast and loud pop music suggest another. We know the significance of the Landrover on the drive outside, the cat purring beside the Aga, the cafetière and croissants before the consumers open their well-fed mouths. Writers of SF and fantasy don't have the option of characterisation by product-placement; the characters we're writing about have a lifestyle totally different from that of their readers. Fantasy writers at least can look to the past for recognisable common references, but the future is unknown territory. Of course, you can describe someone eating rice-flakes in soya milk in a small, over-heated kitchen; but, unless you tell us, we don't know if this signifies poverty or wealth, food-allergies or a taste acquired while serving as cultural attaché to the new Republic on the Moon. People in the future won't talk like us, either, and their physical appearance may be entirely a matter of choice – and may or may not be recognisably human.

So you can't use the usual shortcuts, calling on cultural signifiers which your reader will understand. Instead, everything has to be explained as well as described. But, strip away all the contemporary references, replace them with imagined new details, and you've got people driven by the same basic motives and feelings which have always existed: love, hate, fear, desire; the need to survive, prosper and procreate. Human nature remains the same.

Or does it? Some SF writers would disagree. What *is* human nature? Will it still be recognisable when human beings can download their personalities into little black boxes, or survive for centuries after corporeal death as holographic images? If you take away many of the constraints which have made us what we are – death, birth, life on this planet – and re-imagine us as beings of godlike power, what happens to 'human nature'?

If you're interested in writing SF, you're surely interested in questions like that, and may want to explore them. Good luck. Your challenge will be to keep the reader interested, and to allow them to sympathise with post-human beings.

However, you may prefer to assume, as most SF writers seem to, that people will still be people, whenever and however they live, and describe their actions and emotions accordingly.

Aliens

Another type of character, peculiar to SF, is the alien. The treatment of aliens can generally be broken down into one of three classifications:

- *The Unknowable.* These aliens are utterly inhuman and incomprehensible. The author can only describe, from the outside, an encounter with something absolutely strange. It may be benign, indifferent, or destructive towards humanity, but we don't know why. This classification includes the alien as evil monster to be defeated, and the alien as awe-inspiring godlike being. In either case, the alien functions less as a character, more as a force of nature.
- *Funny Foreigners.* This type of alien has become especially popular ever since the bar scene in *Star Wars* burst upon a happy public. They are the muppets, the computer animations or actors in heavy makeup in every SF TV series or film, and they make appearances in most space operas. Although

not always used as comic relief, and sometimes expected to be taken seriously, these aliens are *character types* rather than fully developed characters. They tend to have one-dimensional personalities, easily described ('Vulcans are highly logical') and at least one strikingly non-human ability or characteristic (telepathy; blue skin; wings). Alternatively, they are *exactly like humans* apart from a few oddities like purple fur, prehensile clawed toes and an unfortunate tendency to burp blue bubbles when startled. It's easy to make fun of them, but they undoubtedly add an appealingly exotic touch to much SF, and can be useful as secondary characters.

• *Strangers*. Some writers make serious attempts to imagine intelligent, non-human life-forms and make them intelligible to their readers. It's a difficult balance to get just right, especially if the aliens are presented as major, viewpoint characters. If they're too strange they'll be impossible to understand or sympathise with; if they're too much like humans they fall into the 'funny foreigner' category and may not be taken seriously. If you want to try going this route, background research into biological sciences and anthropology is useful. The demands are the same as those for serious, extrapolative world-building.

Structure

How much advance planning do you need to do before you start to write? Some writers have everything planned out before they actually write anything: notebooks full of incident and dialogue; folders full of newspaper clippings and photographs; index cards giving background details about every single character; story-boards or chapter breakdowns. At the other extreme are those who don't know what they're going to say until the words appear; they seem to make it up at the keyboard as they go along. One of the questions I'm asked most often is: Should you outline your plot before starting to write a novel?

I used to hate outlines. I've always felt that I learn what I want to write by actually *writing* it. At school, when an outline was required, I used to write my essay *first*, so that I could base the required outline on it, rather than vice versa. I would often start writing a short story with no idea where it was going and find myself pleasantly surprised by the neatness of the ending.

But short stories are one thing – even there, I made a lot of false starts – and novels another. Novels are more complex and take a lot more time to write. The experience of being forced to abandon a novel-in-progress – the slow, painful realisation that it was *not* going to magically 'work out' – is not one I ever want to repeat. It convinced me that although I think of myself as an 'organic' writer – believing that stories develop in more interesting ways if they're allowed to grow, rather than being forced into a rigidly pre-determined scheme – *some* advance planning is necessary. These days I make sure to have a brief synopsis, at least a few paragraphs suggesting the general story, before I begin to write. I may leave the ending open and count on it to come clear as I go along; when I have a final scene in mind before I begin, it usually changes along the way.

How much you want to outline is up to you, but you should have something: a synopsis, a plan, an outline, a treatment – whatever you want to call it. It doesn't have to go into great detail, but it should be written down. This is your map. Even if you never refer to it again, at least you'll know it's there. If you lose your way as you write, or forget what on earth you thought you were doing, your original brief description is there to remind you.

Some people like to outline in more detail, even chapter-by-chapter. There's no doubt that this sort of outlining makes the actual writing go faster, but there's a real risk that if you put too much effort into planning, the writing itself may become a chore, and the final result will be dead on the page.

Beginning

You need to grab the reader's attention on the first page. A kindly editor may give you the benefit of the doubt for two or three pages, but if your opening doesn't compel people to read on, you've lost your one and only chance. A strong first line or paragraph is sometimes referred to as a 'narrative hook'. There are various ways of getting people's attention – sometimes speaking softly can be more effective than shouting – and the approach you take in your first few pages should establish the tone you want to carry throughout the book. A fast-paced, futuristic thriller and a moody, atmospheric dark fantasy will begin in very different ways, but both need to make the reader want to know more.

This is also the place where you'll introduce your reader to your imaginary world. Don't feel you have to do it all at once. Concentrate on the character and the story, and let the details filter through the action, rather than clogging it up with big chunks of exposition and description. It's OK if the reader doesn't know exactly where they are, or understand much about this new world when they begin, as long as their interest is caught. If you feel it is essential to describe your world in detail, this might be better left to the second chapter.

Many fantasy novels open with a *prologue*: a strong, dramatic scene which may have taken place *before* the action of the novel, or which could be a glimpse of something which will happen later in the course of the book. The prologue acts as a sort of 'teaser' to the reader, especially if the first chapter is a quiet one and it is going to take a while for the adventure to really get underway.

Remember, it's not necessary to create the 'perfect' opening in your first draft. When you begin writing your novel or story, you are writing first and foremost for yourself. After you've written the first draft (or occasionally, as I've found, halfway through it) you'll have a much better idea of what would make the best opening scene. Sometimes you'll find that the ending will change your mind completely about the beginning. Even if you are absolutely certain how your story must begin, you'll want to polish it later.

Middle

This is the bulk of the book, where plot and characters are both developed and complicated on the way towards the conclusion.

There are no hard-and-fast rules for developing your plot, but here are a few things to think about:

- *Coincidence.* Yes, chance does play a large role in real life, and that's why people say that truth is stranger than fiction. We look for a satisfying order in fiction, not often to be found in life. Unless your story is actually *about* coincidence (a scientist who learns how to predict it, for example), better avoid it. Although, curiously, readers are usually more willing to accept the malign working of coincidence – life making things tougher for the hero – than the notion of a lucky break. However, important plot complications should result from actions taken by the main characters, or logically from the situation you've established.
- *Play fair with the reader.* Anything can happen in fantasy, but total chaos is dramatically unsatisfying. Whether you're writing about magic or science, it must have rules – and it's your duty to communicate these rules to the reader. If there are flying carpets or matter-transmitters in your invented world, we should know about them well before the hero pulls one out of his bag to make a daring escape.
- *The 'idiot plot'.* This is the plot that only works because people behave like idiots: the hero forgets to take basic precautions, blabs to the enemy, goes back to the haunted house after dark all alone, etc. It is clumsy and annoying. Avoid it.
- *Theme.* SF and fantasy novels can be moral dramas with important themes at the same time as they are entertaining adventure stories. They are perfect vehicles for investigating big questions such as: How can society be changed for the better? What is the nature of intelligence? What does it mean to be human? Does absolute evil exist? The most memorable SF and fantasy lingers in the mind because it is *about* something more than just the plot – it makes the reader think. Although it is possible to write purely for entertainment, this genre offers greater possibilities, and it's worth keeping that in mind as you work out your plot. Certain types of story may express your theme better than others. Usually you will discover your theme

after you've started to write, rather than having it firmly fixed in mind when you begin. Don't worry if you think you have no theme – your readers may find one anyway.

End

Upbeat, positive endings are preferred by most readers and editors of popular fiction. It's true that there is a tradition of downbeat, even downright grim endings in SF, particularly when it is dystopian (think of *1984*), and sometimes these are essential. Another possibility (a favourite of mine) is the ambiguous ending which can be read in more than one way. However, most popular fantasy and SF has a 'feel-good' factor, and a satisfying, upbeat conclusion is part of that. Most readers want to see the heroine or hero win through and triumph at the end. This doesn't mean that all endings must be unrelievedly happy; there can be death, sadness, even defeat. An ending may still be perceived as being positive as long as defeat is not total. Lives and happiness may have been sacrificed to a greater good; the hero or heroine may be sadder but wiser, looking ahead to new possibilities. Grim and gloomy short stories are fine, but readers usually prefer to be left with a sense of hope and an uplifted feeling when they finish a novel.

Writers are often advised to avoid *deus ex machina* endings. The term – literally, in Latin, 'a god from a machine' – refers to the resolution of plot-problems by supernatural or other extraordinary means. This is unbelievable in mainstream, realistic fiction: however, SF is often metaphysical in nature, so endings in which humanity acquires godlike powers, or makes contact with godlike aliens, are not uncommon. Supernatural or magical resolutions to fantasy novels are acceptable as long as you play fair with the reader. Magical solutions should have been demonstrated or hinted at earlier in the plot – the resolution shouldn't seem to come out of nowhere – and must be in keeping with the rest of the novel. The important thing is that the ending should feel integral to the whole, *earned* by the characters, and therefore satisfying, rather than a cop-out from an author unable to work out anything better.

5
Language: Viewpoint and Style

As I pointed out in the previous chapter, every character has his or her own story, and one of the major questions to ask in working out a plot is: Whose story is it? Even when you know whose story you want to tell, there is something else you must decide – who's telling it?

Who's telling the story?

Every work of fiction has a narrator. The relationship between the narrator and the story – in other words, how the story is told – is referred to as the 'point of view' (sometimes abbreviated to POV). The narrator is either a character in the story – the *viewpoint character* – or an authorial voice.

There are basically three narrative points of view: *first person*, *limited third person*, and what may be called *omniscient author*. Some stories have been written using the second person ('you') – an example would be something like:

> You're on the run. You're scared. Somehow, they've found
> out where you live, so you can't go home. If they catch
> you, they'll kill you. You feel like crying, but you know
> you have to stay calm and try to outwit them.

This rarely used point of view may be considered as a variant of the first person. It reflects the way people sometimes speak, using 'you' as a way of generalising, rather than admitting that they are talking about themselves ('You get kind of nervous when you think people are looking at you, you know?') and is best avoided as a way of telling a story. Use first or third person instead.

First person

It was a cold, clear day and the air tasted faintly of apples. Since the ground was not too muddy, I soon left the road and struck off across the fields. I was travelling to the east of the house, up a hill, and the exertion of climbing soon had me feeling warm and vigorous. When I reached the top of the hill I paused to catch my breath and survey the countryside. Our house was easily picked out because it stood away from the village, amid fields and farmland, and my eyes went to it at once. The sight of it made me smile, made me feel proud, as if it were something I had made and not merely bought. There were the yellow stones of my house; there the bright green patch of the untended garden; there the spiky winter trees standing close to the east wall, like guardians.

I squinted and pressed my glasses further up my nose, closer to my eyes, unable to believe what I saw. There was something large and black in one of the trees; something that reminded me horribly of a man crouching there, spying on the house. Absurd, it couldn't be – but there *was* something there, something much bigger than a rook or a cat. Something that did not belong; something dangerous.

This example of first-person point of view is from my short story, 'The Nest'. I wrote it in first person because the story could not have been told in any other way. 'The Nest' is a psychological horror story about the fears, fantasies and family relationships of one woman, the main character. As she describes them, ordinary events become weirdly horrifying. The narrator sees things that no one else sees, and she reaches frightening conclusions. The suspense in the story is all to do with the narrator's mental processes and the reader's awareness of her oddity; if she didn't tell her own story, it would not exist.

The first-person point of view is particularly useful when you want to keep your story ambiguous: did it really happen, or was the narrator fantasising ... or mad? *The Turn of the Screw* by Henry James is a brilliant example; so is *The Affirmation* by Christopher Priest.

However, the use of first person doesn't have to be ambiguous or unreliable; it can also be perfectly straightforward. There's a long-standing tradition of tales of exploration and adventure told in the first person by honest, reliable blokes. First person can be a good choice when you want the reader to come to a gradual understanding, having an experience in tandem with the main character. It can be effective in the sort of fantasy in which a secondary world is entered from our own.

Cross-Stitch by Diana Gabaldon is a fantasy-romance in which a young woman is abruptly catapulted from her life in the 1940s into the Highlands of Scotland in the 1740s. The young woman, Claire, tells her own story. Since she's no expert on history, her experience of learning about the situation she's found herself in parallels that of the reader. Having worked as a nurse in the Second World War, she's competent, tough-minded and adaptable; since she takes her own competence for granted, the reader also accepts it. And, because she is open about her emotions, her fears and her failings, she never comes across as an unbelievable superwoman. Readers have no problem imagining themselves in Claire's place.

If you want to concentrate on one main character, having this person actually tell the story may be the right choice. An interesting and original 'voice' can make a story fresh and com-pelling. Some writers are drawn to the first-person narrator almost instinctively; others, like actors, enjoy adopting a variety of voices and taking on different roles; while still others will only use 'I' for a fictional character very like themselves.

There *are* limitations to writing in the first person. Everything has to be filtered through the one viewpoint, restricted to what the narrator might plausibly know or understand. Other characters may seem one-dimensional by comparison. However, this particular limitation can actually work *for* you in short stories where there isn't room to develop a lot of different characters. The only scenes which can be described are those in which your narrator is involved – again, this is something which is a plus in a short story. In a novel, plot problems may arise as you struggle to manoeuvre your character into the right place at the right time to witness some vital bit of drama (my pet peeve is the long, intimate scene improbably witnessed by a character lurking in the shadows), or you may find yourself forced into too many undramatic summaries of off-stage events. And you must stay in character at all times. Middle-aged authors must be careful not to make their teenaged narrators too wise and experienced; equally, younger authors shouldn't make the mistake of assuming that 50-year-olds will have the same take on life as themselves.

Another thing to bear in mind is 'doting parent syndrome'. You may be madly in love with your main character, but that's no guarantee that the rest of the world will be equally adoring. Cute habits can become annoying after 100-plus pages. If a viewpoint character is perceived as 'unsympathetic' – even when that is the author's intention – readers may not stick with the book. It's one thing to read a book about a misogynistic psychopath, distanced by authorial objectivity; quite another to have him whispering his life story in your ear.

Limited third person

Third person is 'he' or 'she' or, if you're telling the story of a machine-intelligence or other ungendered being, 'it'. 'Limited' refers to the author's decision to stick to the limits of what one character experiences. In this way it is similar to the first-person narrator, and imposes the same limitations. Sometimes, when the view is kept very tightly focused on what the main character experiences, first and third person are practically indistinguishable. (You can check it out for yourself by going through a story and swapping every 'I', 'me' and 'mine' for third-person pronouns. Does the new version read comfortably? Or does that one simple change make the story feel wrong, or false, or in crying need of a complete revision?)

80

The use of third person rather than first offers at least the illusion of objectivity. Although we are told what the main character thinks and feels (and none of the other characters get this treatment), this information comes not in the character's own words, but from outside, from a higher authority – the author. A first-person narrator can only write subjectively, and may be utterly unreliable as a witness, but readers expect that what is told in third person will be the objective (if fictional) truth. However, as long as you are sticking with *limited* third person, rather than taking on the voice of the omniscient author, what readers are told must be filtered through the perceptions of the viewpoint character, without overt authorial judgement or comment. Limited third person can be as subjective and restricted as first-person narration. Other characters are perceived only in relation to the viewpoint character, who must be present in every scene.

Omniscient author

Some writers don't like the term 'omniscient' – perhaps it sounds too godlike? But all authors are omniscient: after all, it's your story, your world; you made it up and must therefore know everything there is to know about it. That doesn't mean you need to keep reminding your readers of your omniscience.

The viewpoint of the omniscient author may be more helpfully considered as a continuum which stretches from the intrusive author at one end to the detached author at the other. The intrusive/omniscient author tells you everything about everybody, and judges them:

> In a month's time, Lucy would be dead. But now, bliss-
> fully unaware of her fate, she iced Joe's birthday cake,
> humming happily to herself. The simple task freed her
> mind to ponder questions of higher philosophy. She was
> on course to win her university's top prize with her latest
> essay. Joe watched greedily, gazing at Lucy's plump
> bottom and wondering if she was wearing any under-
> pants. He should have been attending to his own work,

81

the broken transformer bleeping urgently at him from the kitchen table, but, as usual, he was too easily distracted by the needs of the flesh. That momentary lapse of attention would cost him dear, although he would never know why. Unseen by either Lucy or Joe, the cat, feeling bored, climbed into the oven and curled up for a nap.

There may be questions or comments directed to the reader – bits of advice or small sermons:

> Now, gentle reader, let this be a lesson to you, as it was to our foolish heroine! Never leave your oven door open when there's a cat around!

Victorian novelists, in particular, felt comfortable stepping in and out of their story to address the reader directly, but this has generally fallen into disfavour. Although some postmodern writers, including Joanna Russ and Fay Weldon, have handled the intrusive-omniscient voice with a witty effectiveness, it is something to be attempted only with extreme care. Unless you know what you are doing, and have a very good reason for it, you're advised to steer clear of this style.

At the other extreme is the detached author, or what might be described as the 'camera's eye view' – the pretence is that the author has no special inside knowledge but is simply a reporter, describing a scene to you in the same way that a machine might record what happens, without comment or judgement. This attempts to dispense with any viewpoint character; to tell a story by simply, neutrally describing what is happening. The reader can only guess at what characters are thinking and feeling by what they say and do, and from descriptions of their appearance. Some very cool, minimalist SF has been written from this 'non-viewpoint', but the story has to be very strong to sustain it at any length. This viewpoint is deliberately distancing, so the reader may find it hard to become involved enough to care. And although it can be a relief from overheated, overblown emotional melodrama, it is equally unreal, and can be frustrating to the reader.

What might be called the 'modified omniscient' viewpoint or 'involved author' falls somewhere in the middle. The omniscience of the involved author – who exists above and beyond all the viewpoint characters, and admits to knowing the whole story – is demonstrated in the works of writers such as Dickens and Tolstoy, as well as in the folksier realm of the classic fairy tale. However, modern authors tend to feel less comfortable with such an openly omniscient viewpoint. More common is what Dean Koontz has called the 'modified omniscient' viewpoint. This gives a broader scope than either the first person or the limited third person, allowing for more complex story-lines and generally more textural richness. I would guess that the majority of popular, successful fantasy and SF novels are written using modified omniscience. This gives the author the freedom to move among a variety of different viewpoint characters rather than sticking with one. Information and descriptions don't have to be filtered through a character's perceptions, but can be presented directly by the author without apology – whether this means describing an empty room, or providing a brief historical background of an imaginary kingdom. Here's an example, from the opening of *The Dispossessed* by Ursula K. LeGuin:

There was a wall. It did not look important. It was built of uncut rocks roughly mortared. An adult could look right over it, and even a child could climb it. Where it crossed the roadway, instead of having a gate it degenerated into mere geometry, a line, an idea of boundary. But the idea was real. It was important. For seven generations there had been nothing in the world more important than that wall.

Like all walls it was ambiguous, two-faced. What was inside it and what was outside it depended upon which side of it you were on.

Looked at from one side, the wall enclosed a barren sixty-acre field called the Port of Anarres. On the field there were a couple of large gantry cranes, a rocket pad, three warehouses, a truck garage, and a dormitory. The dormitory looked durable, grimy, and mournful; it had no gardens, no children; plainly nobody lived there or was even meant to stay there long. It was in fact a quarantine. The wall shut in not only the landing field but also the ships that came down out of space, and the men that came on the ships, and the worlds they came from, and the rest of the universe. It enclosed the universe, leaving Anarres outside, free.

Looked at from the other side, the wall enclosed Anarres: the whole planet was inside it, a great prison camp, cut off from other worlds and other men, in quarantine.

A number of people were coming along the road towards the landing field, or standing around where the road cut through the wall.

The description continues with the mood of the crowd, who have come watch, to protest against – some, to attempt to kill – a man who is about to leave Anarres. Two pages later we are with this man, Shevek, who is the main viewpoint character of the novel.

Switching viewpoints

Technically, the omniscient-author viewpoint gives you the freedom to move in and out of all the characters' points of view, from hero or heroine to sidekick to villain to onlooker to the cat under the table. For each character, the story is subtly (or substantially) different, and whom you choose as your viewpoint character will to a large extent determine the story you tell. By giving us the emotions and thoughts of several different characters, instead of only one, you can reveal more about motivations and attitudes, show the wider-ranging effect of actions and produce a more sophisticated story. But this freedom must be handled with care.

Every time you change your viewpoint character, you should be aware that you're doing it – and have a reason for the shift.

In general, you should *not* switch viewpoints in a single scene; certainly not in the same paragraph, as I did in my bad example, above, about Lucy and Joe and the cat. If you do, you're going to jar the reader, disrupt the illusion the fiction has created, and draw attention to the heavy-handed author.

Always be aware of who your viewpoint character is, and stick with that one throughout a given scene. If information about another character's feelings is important, it must be transmitted through the thoughts or perceptions of the viewpoint character:

> As she turned around, Lucy saw Joe hastily raise his eyes. He looked guilty. He's been staring at my bottom, Lucy thought, startled. She hoped she wasn't blushing, and tried to smile in a normal sort of way as she handed him a spoon.

Switching from one viewpoint to another very frequently is a tricky thing to handle. It's jarring for the reader, so you need to signal your intention in advance. Momentary viewpoint shifts are usually a mistake; all too often the author isn't even aware of doing it. One common mistake is to describe the viewpoint character *from the outside.* Just as a first-person narrator is unlikely to say, 'I narrowed my beautiful brown eyes in anger', so references to the viewpoint character in terms expressing an onlooker's point of view also feel wrong. If Lucy is your viewpoint character, she may *think* that she's blushing, or her face may feel warm, but saying 'she turned red' or 'her cheeks reddened' implies the point of view of someone other than Lucy. Of course, this 'other' may be the omniscient author, who is perfectly justified in giving such external descriptions along with an insight into Lucy's thoughts. But unless you are in complete control of the omniscient authorial voice, and maintain it smoothly and consistently, the reader may get the impression of being jerked roughly out of one viewpoint for some more or less pointless comment before being shoved back in again. This is tiring, and does not inspire confidence in the reader.

It's best to give a clear signal when you mean to switch from one viewpoint to another. There's no need to do anything terribly dramatic – to change typeface, or head the page with the new character's name – unless you want to. The chapters in George R. R. Martin's *A Game of Thrones* are given the names of their viewpoint characters. In *Revelation Space* by Alistair Reynolds, two separate plots, with a different cast of characters, run parallel in the same chapters, separated only by line-breaks. As long as you're clear and consistent, you can deal with a large number of viewpoint characters without confusion. But unless you have a very good reason for it, and are sure you've handled the transitions smoothly, it's best to avoid viewpoint changes in mid-scene.

As a rule of thumb, if you want to switch your viewpoint character, wait for the break. The pause at the end of a chapter, or even a line-break between scenes on one page, is enough to prepare the reader for the change.

Shifts between different limited-third-person viewpoints are the most common of viewpoint changes. Although short stories should generally be limited to one – or at most two – points of view, novels, and especially longer, more complex novels, often benefit from having more than one viewpoint character. How many is up to you, and depends on the sort of story you want to tell. There's no law that says the chapters have to be evenly divided, or the viewpoint characters equally represented. It's not necessary to repeat the same scene through the eyes of your two (or more) main viewpoint characters – in fact, unless it's vital to make the point about how different the same events can appear to different people, it's better *not* to repeat scenes or information.

Changing between first person and third person is trickier, and less commonly done. Sometimes the device of a diary, letters, or some other sort of written testament – a book within a book – is used. Or you may want to write some chapters in the first person, others in third person from the viewpoint of a different character, as I did in my novel *Gabriel*.

Originally I had intended to write *Gabriel* entirely in third person. It was primarily Dinah's story, but because I wanted the reader to have access to information that wasn't available to her,

I knew I would need at least one other limited-third-person viewpoint character. That turned out to be a little boy, Ben. Most of the story was Dinah's, and it was a very internal, emotional story focused on her desires and fears. When I was about 80 pages in, I began to feel that I couldn't go on. The story was dead on the page. I was in despair; I thought I'd have to give up. As a last resort, I decided to try letting Dinah tell her own story, and I began all over again, writing in the first person – and, to my relief, delight and astonishment, the book came to life.

But the need for a second viewpoint character remained. I considered letting Ben tell his own story, but wasn't satisfied with with my nine-year-old's first-person voice: I was too aware of how much he couldn't, or wouldn't, say. So I wrote five of the 15 chapters that made up the novel in limited third person, from Ben's point of view.

Novels with more than one first-person viewpoint narrator are not common, but if you do want to try it, be sure to keep your 'I's distinct. Not only do they need to be presented in clearly separated sections (I can't imagine anything but chaos if you tried to move between two first-person narrators in the same scene!), but they should ideally have distinctly different voices, and be quite different personalities.

Switching between first-person and limited-third-person viewpoints when the two are the same character, or between first person and omniscient author, is unusual, and most likely to be done for a very specific stylistic purpose – such as a comment on the act of writing, as a way of indicating mental instability in the narrator, or to reveal that the viewpoint character has more than one persona (which is not the same thing as madness). For an example of the last, see my *Lost Futures*, or Kate Wilhelm's *Margaret and I*.

Style

Style is what makes each author unique. It's readily recognisable, and parodied, yet it can be nearly invisible – the 'clear pane of glass' effect to which many modern writers aspire. But what is it? Discuss the 'style' of a story, and it seems as if you're talking about something quite separate from the content. You may have played the game of taking a well-known story – say, 'Goldilocks and the Three Bears' – and rewriting it in the style of some well-known writer. Parodies work because writers have their own distinctive, imitable styles. Terry Pratchett's 'Goldilocks' would be utterly different from Stephen King's 'Porridge'.

And yet, to a large extent, the style *is* the story. Strip away style, and what's left is a bare plot synopsis – not a story, and certainly not a novel. 'Put in opposition to "style", there is no such thing as "content",' Samuel R. Delany once wrote: 'Is there such a thing as verbal information apart from the words used to inform?'

Young writers are often encouraged to find their own style, and much of a writer's development is just that – the development of an individual, workable style. But style is not something that can be worked on in isolation. It's something that will develop while you write; not something you can impose on a mass of inchoate material ('story'), but rather an aspect of the stories you want to write – an expression of your own writerly personality, the way in which you perceive and describe the world.

Certain kinds of stories seem to set their own agendas as far as style is concerned; you ignore the demands of the material at your peril. If you write a story about princesses, dragons and magic rings in the style of Ernest Hemingway, for example, you may have an interesting story, but it is unlikely to feel much like fantasy.

The best essay I can think of on the subject of style and fantasy is 'From Elfland to Poughkeepsie' by Ursula K. LeGuin. I urge you to find a copy and read it. Although the market for commercial fantasy has expanded hugely since she wrote her essay in 1973, everything she said then is still relevant today.

Because it is different from realistic, naturalistic fiction, something other than a realistic, naturalistic style seems called for in fantasy. Sometimes a deliberately plain and ordinary style can be effective in heightening the strangeness when a story concerns the eruption of the fantastic into our world, or is about

88

ordinary people confronting the extraordinary. SF writers often strive for a clear, unambiguous style to make their amazing ideas more acceptable. However, when a story is set in another world – whether Middle Earth, Elfland, or in a Galaxy far, far away – we want to feel the strangeness of it. A distancing effect can be used to emphasise that this world is not *our* world, and that the people who inhabit it are different from our neighbours. Distance and difference are invoked in language, by the style in which the story is told.

High fantasy

Some people feel that heroic or high fantasy is best written in an elaborate, old-fashioned style. Lord Dunsany (1878–1957) is a writer often cited as an example of the archaic, high-fantasy style at its best. Here's a sample from the first chapter of *The King of Elfland's Daughter*:

'My people demand a magic lord to rule over them. They have chosen foolishly,' the old lord said, 'and only the Dark Ones that show not their faces know all that this will bring: but we, who see not, follow the ancient custom and do what our people in their parliament say. It may be some spirit of wisdom they have not known may save them even yet. Go then with your face turned towards that light that beats from fairyland, and that faintly illumines the dusk between sunset and early stars, and this shall guide you till you come to the frontier and have passed the fields we know.'

Then he unbuckled a strap and a girdle of leather and gave his huge sword to his son, saying: 'This that has brought our family down the ages unto this day shall surely guard you always upon your journey, even though you fare beyond the fields we know.'

And the young man took it though he knew that no such sword could avail him.

Near the Castle of Erl there lived a lonely witch, on high land near the thunder, which used to roll in Summer along the hills. There she dwelt by herself in a narrow cottage of thatch and roamed the high fields alone to gather the thunderbolts. Of these thunderbolts, that had no earthly forging, were made, with suitable runes, such weapons as had to parry unearthly dangers.

LeGuin is an admirer of Dunsany, whom she describes as 'the most imitated, and the most inimitable, writer of fantasy' and also as 'the First Terrible Fate that Awaiteth Unwary Beginners in Fantasy'.

Dunsany's style – influenced by the King James Bible and Irish speech rhythms, both of which he heard from his earliest years – was very much his own, and perfectly suited for the poetic fantasies he wrote with an equally outmoded quill pen. He was deliberately old-fashioned, and he knew what he was doing. The archaic style flowed naturally for him; like it or not (I'm not a big fan, myself), it doesn't ring false.

The problem with attempting a style like Dunsany's, or like E. R. Eddison's in *The Worm Ouroboros*, or Malory's *Morte d'Arthur* (written in the 15th century) is that it's very difficult for a modern writer to do it convincingly. Your ear must be absolutely true: as with poetry, one slip can destroy the whole. Make a single mistake and the whole thing will sound fake. Prose may fall flat if it sounds too colloquial and every-day, but fake archaic language is even worse. Fantasy writers are best advised to strive to achieve a style which is neither ostentatiously old-fashioned nor bursting with contemporary catch-phrases, but which is both elegant and modern; with luck and care it may seem timeless.

Plain prose

In 'From Elfland to Poughkeepsie', LeGuin points out that most epics and sagas, whether prose or verse, were written in straightforward language, simple and clear. 'A plain language is the noblest of all,' she writes. 'It is also the most difficult.'

Robin Scott Wilson founded the Clarion Writers' Workshop (which I attended in 1971 and 1972) where he offered us 'Wilson's Four Rules of Good Writing':

1. Never use a big word if a little one will do.
2. Never use two words where one will do.
3. Avoid the passive voice like the plague.
4. Let the verbs carry the load.

Variations on these rules often appear in writers' guides, and they can be helpful as a reminder of the virtues of simplicity. If you're in love with words, it can be easy to let yourself get carried away by sound rather than sense, or to forget about the need for clarity and communication. I myself am a great admirer of clarity and simplicity in writing, but the rules above – like all 'rules for writing' – should frequently be ignored. (Except possibly for rule number 3!) Literature would be much impoverished if all writers stripped their sentences to the bone. There's nothing wrong with a 'big word' when it's the *right* word. Wilson's rules, it seems to me now, are a recipe for a very superior journalistic prose – fine, as far as it goes, but limited.

Dialogue

How will people of the future talk? How do you converse with an alien?

At first, dialogue seems like a particularly knotty problem for the writer of fantasy and science fiction. Whether you're writing about the inhabitants of some fantastic other-world, or far-future citizens of the galaxy, you really don't want your characters to talk exactly like the people of today. On the other hand, you want your readers to sympathise and even identify with them, which means they have to speak a recognisable, comprehensible form of English which comes across as believable. They should sound different, but not silly.

'Naturalistic' dialogue is a convention. The way people speak in fiction is not the way people talk in real life. You'll find this for yourself if you record a small group of friends talking in the pub or around a dinner table, and then transcribe it. Real conversation is full of pauses, repetitions, broken sentences and body language. Fiction which attempted to reproduce the reality of talk would be too tedious to read. Even writers renowned for writing grittily realistic dialogue take liberties and play artistic tricks (using repetition and colourful slang, for example) to achieve their effect. Most readers prefer fictional characters who are more fluent than most people in real life.

Dialogue in fantasy-fiction offers a much wider scope than that in realistic fiction. You may treat it the way some historical writers do, as if you were translating from another language into modern English, and get away with using entirely contemporary idioms and even slang. Or you may want to suggest a completely different style of speaking: depending on the society you envision, this might be extremely florid and full of elaborate phrases, or stripped-down and economical. It might be peppered with invented words, or allusive and poetic. Experiment to find out what suits your world and your style and story the best.

It's important to remember that people speak in different ways in different contexts (people use different vocabulary according to whether they're speaking to children, employers, friends, servants or clients), and that character traits are often expressed in speech. Make sure that all your characters don't sound exactly alike.

There's no reason to assume that aliens would necessarily have a spoken language. They might communicate through colours or smells or body-postures. This can be used for humorous effect, or simply as another detail to make their alien-ness more complete and convincing. However, if they're going to be important characters, you need to work out some efficient way of 'translating' their non-verbal conversation so it doesn't bring the story grinding to a halt as the poor reader struggles to make sense of it all.

Experiment. Be inventive, and have fun – but don't lose sight of the fact that dialogue in fantasy and SF must do its usual fictional work of advancing the plot, developing characters and keeping the reader entertained.

Future language

Fantasy writers may look to the past – to epic literature, historical documents, and archaic terminology – to forge their prose style, but how do you write about the future?

A plain, clear, flexible language is a good start. If you write in a modern, contemporary-sounding style, that is likely to seem appropriate for SF. As critics have pointed out before, SF writers are actually writing about the present. Be careful in your use of very contemporary slang, though – that will date your story fast. Making up words can be tricky, but it's fun. Language does change; sometimes new words come into existence (neologisms), but sometimes old words are brought back into usage for new concepts. What will people call whatever replaces television? Neither 'Holovision' nor 'Tri-vid' have ever sounded convincing to me, although so many writers have used them they've taken on their own sort of reality. Will 'TV' and 'telly' soon sound as quaint as 'wireless' does now? I was startled to hear my 13-year-old daughter referring to her CDs as 'records' – she's never even *seen* the black vinyl discs that were 'records' to me!

The idea of using an elaborate word like 'facsimile' – even reduced as it was to 'fax' – struck me as odd when 'faxes' first appeared on the scene. I would have thought it unconvincing if it had appeared in an SF novel! I was so taken with the word that I used it for my own purposes in a story called 'Memories of the Body'. Instead of a piece of paper, a 'fax' in my fictional world was a sort of android – a duplicate person.

Rare, archaic and elaborate words can be used to imbue a distant, far future with an interesting, almost-but-not-quite recognisable strangeness. For a good example of this, check out *Appleseed* by John Clute.

Settlers on far worlds, like explorers and settlers on our own, are likely to name the flora and fauna after striking characteristics ('red-throated warbler') or after a resemblance to something at home ('robins' or 'bread-fruit') rather than inventing totally new words for them. Of course, if there are aliens with their own language on these far worlds, that's a whole new ball-game.

Some writers have invented dialects in which to write their novels of the future – Anthony Burgess did it in *A Clockwork Orange* and Russell Hoban in *Riddley Walker*. The potential which science fiction offers to recreate not only our world, but also the language in which we write about it, is one of the genre's most challenging attractions.

Alien names

Some people glory in making them up, others in making fun of them. There's nothing to guarantee that your made-up names won't be laughed at by somebody, somewhere; but to help you avoid unintentional humour, here's a few helpful hints:

- Read your names aloud. Did you do it without stumbling? Did any of them make you giggle? Avoid impossible strings of letters.
- Raid foreign dictionaries and atlases. Slightly altered place-names can often work as personal names. Basing all your names on one particular language can have the positive effect of making them sound consistent. If your characters came from earth long, long before, their names might plausibly be corruptions of Swedish or Urdu words; however, frog creatures from another galaxy should not be named after French towns. Also, take note of what the words you're borrowing really mean, and don't use anything too obvious; I've never been allowed to forget the time I named a character after a well-known Spanish dessert ...
- Use apostrophes and other punctuation as they were intended – don't just stick them in anywhere to make an ordinary word look weird.

Expository lumps

That's what they called them when I went to Clarion in the early 1970s; nowadays the preferred terminology seems to be 'info-dumps'. Or 'TMI' – short for 'Too Much Information'!

An expository lump, or info-dump, is basically a chunk of explanation which draws attention to itself. The story comes to a halt while this information is transmitted. Although expository lumps may turn up in any genre, they are a particular problem in SF, where the reader may need to understand some basic scientific laws before the story will make any sense.

There are various ways of disguising expository lumps. That clichéd figure from old SF movies, the scientist's beautiful daughter, was a useful stand-in for the ignorant audience as her father explained the situation in simple terms. Turning a lecture into a conversation is another guise, although lines beginning, 'As you know ...' are a dead give-away that this conversation exists solely to enlighten the reader.

Another type of info-dump occurs without apology because of the didactic nature of some SF. Some writers have always enjoyed the role of prophet or teacher, and use SF not only to entertain, but to instruct. And many SF readers, especially fans of hard SF, do like to learn from their reading, and are curious about the science behind the fiction.

Brian Stableford is one SF writer who admits that he is often at odds with editors who argue that his stories are sometimes too much like lectures. Stableford writes:

> 'I honestly believe that many sf readers actually appreciate a bit of background information now and again, and will forgive the occasional interruption of the action. Even in those of my novels which I remember with pride, therefore, the reader is apt to stumble across long, deep conversations, or chunks excerpted from imaginary reference books.'*

*Stableford, *The Way to Write Science Fiction*

There are no hard-and-fast rules; you must discover, by doing, what works best for you (and whether it will work for readers). Try to be aware of what you are doing, and what effect you want to achieve – if not at the first-draft stage, then certainly when you rewrite. And, while listening to editorial advice, remember that you can't please everyone.

Imitation

Style is an individual thing, and it develops over time. The young writer, especially, may test and discard many different approaches before settling on one that works. Don't be afraid of sounding too much like someone else in your quest to improve. Not only is imitation the sincerest form of flattery, it is also a great way to learn.

When I was very young, I was always writing stories in imitation of whatever impressed me in my reading. Even in my early 20s, when I was a published author, I would occasionally make a deliberate attempt to write a story in the style of a writer I particularly admired. I think most writers do this – certainly, my friends and contemporaries have all admitted to it. There is no way to learn about writing except by writing, and if you have something to model yourself against, it can help you figure out why one thing 'works' and another doesn't, how certain effects are achieved, and just how style is inseparable from content.

So go ahead and imitate. Treat it as an exercise. Choose something you wish that you had written, and try to work out how it was done by writing something similar.

Collaboration can be helpful, too. It's not for everyone, but I found that working with another writer taught me a lot about different approaches to the same material, and the way in which a story can grow in unexpected directions. The experience of rewriting someone else's work – and having them do the same to you – is particularly eye-opening.

6
Rewriting

You must write, and then you must rewrite. Rewriting is crucial. Some writers love the act of writing, the rush of creativity, the total freedom of making everything up, but find rewriting a chore. They are full of ideas, and as soon as they've finished a story they lose interest and are eager to move on to something else. Rewriting feels like a waste of time. So much to say! So little time! Iain Banks has admitted that he felt like that for years – but he also pointed out that *The Wasp Factory*, the first novel he sold, was also the first novel he'd taken the time to rewrite.

For me, the first draft is the hard work, and rewriting is the fun part. I like to make a comparison between fiction writing and sculpture – the sculptor begins with raw material like a block of marble or wood, and carves it into the desired shape. But the fiction writer has to produce the raw material itself, and only then can begin to chip and smooth and sand and polish it into a story or a novel.

Like the old lady who didn't know what she meant to say until she saw what she'd said, I find out what my story is by writing it. I think on the keyboard. Naturally, I make mistakes. I may take the wrong turning, plot-wise, or write scenes which go on for too long – possibly revealing some useful insights into my characters, but not advancing the story. These need to be cut from the finished work, but it's wrong to think of all those pages as either unnecessary or a waste of time. I had to write them, write *through* them, to find out what I wanted to say, and to get where I was going. Sometimes, on the other hand, I'll be so impatient to get to the end that I'll leave out important details, skipping over scenes which provide necessary background information. Often, I'll write awkwardly or vaguely, just to move along to the next page. There's no point in feeling self-conscious about a badly written first draft: this is just the sketch, the groundwork that no one else is meant to see.

Not everyone works like this. There are writers whose first drafts are of publishable quality. For some, this is because they've lived through, worked out or visualised their story in detail before writing it down; others may have brooded over their ideas for weeks, months or even years. Some simply can't bear to write the second sentence until they feel certain that the first is as perfect as they can make it; they build their stories line-by-line and if each sentence, each paragraph, is solid and right, and slots neatly into the next, the result will be sound and complete – in no more need of rewriting than a well-constructed house or wall is in need of being rebuilt. Some writers, like some speakers, seem 'naturally' fluent and polished. Usually this apparent ease demonstrates a natural ability combined with hard work and years of practice – as with gymnasts and athletes, it's not as easy as it looks. The hard work may be invisible to the outsider, but it is there. Harlan Ellison has turned writing into a spectator sport, making public appearances (sometimes actually in a bookshop window) during which he writes short stories on demand. Stephen King is another writer who enjoys challenging himself – like a tightrope-walker working without a net – by publishing sections of works-in-progress; and of course Charles Dickens did that long before King was born.

Kids, don't try this at home! If you're an unpublished writer, my advice to you is to write and then rewrite. And then rewrite your work yet again, and read it through very carefully and critically before you submit anything for publication.

Two types of rewriting

There are two types of rewriting: *polishing* and *revision*. Nearly all first drafts will benefit from the first; not all need the second. Here's an example of polishing (or tinkering) at work: the first time I wrote the above sentence, it was 'Nearly all first drafts will benefit from the first type; not all will require the second.' On re-reading, I decided that was too wordy and made changes.

The widespread use of word-processing programmes has blurred the distinction of the first draft. Unless you write in long-hand, or on an old-fashioned typewriter, even talking about 'first draft' – as distinct from second, third or fourth – can seem a rather arbitrary distinction. Like many writers, I usually start my day's work by rewriting what I did the day before, and occasionally I decide that major changes are necessary before I can continue. By the time I've reached the end of what I still think of as the 'first draft' of a short story or novel, much of it will have been edited on-screen and rewritten at least once, parts of it possibly two or three times, making it technically a second or third draft.

Back in the 1970s, long before the days of PCs and e-mail, when I used to get letters from George R.R. Martin typed on odd-sized sheets of paper, it was a sign that he was working hard. To avoid having to retype the whole manuscript, George, like a lot of writers then, used to type up the new material, cut it out, and paste it over the crossed-out text he'd decided to delete. That was the origin of the 'cut and paste' functions in word-processing programmes – only now the seams are invisible.

There's no doubt that computers have made life easier for writers. Small changes are so simple – adding whole sentences is easier than crossing out a single word used to be. There's no excuse for not doing it. I remember when a common question asked of editors was how many hand-written changes were acceptable before the whole page had to be retyped; small changes were *agonised* over. Now, you can do it and undo it with a minimum of physical effort, and it all looks so *good*. No one will know whether a particularly apt description or witty line leapt fully formed from brain to page, or was changed three, six or 26 different times in an authorial quest for perfection.

But although working on a computer has made polishing so much easier, it can actually be a hindrance when it comes to revision.

The curse of the computer

If you're in the habit of writing and rewriting directly onto a computer – comfortable cutting and pasting, saving and deleting, shifting blocks of text around, using 'find and replace' like a good little robot to change characters' names, and using spell-checkers and search functions and all that – you may shudder at the very idea of doing without your cybernetic servant. There are still writers who write by hand or even use old-fashioned typewriters, but I certainly wouldn't want to go back to starting over on a fresh sheet of paper every time I wanted to change a few lines.

Yet there's something about the way in which text seems endlessly malleable on the screen that can be a trap. Because you don't have to retype the whole lot – the good with the bad – it tends to be only the obvious errors which compel your attention. Those are the only parts that you change. Concentrating on the little things, you may miss larger, less obvious flaws. Working on bits and pieces out of context means you may miss the way changes made in one part of the story affect the whole thing. Tinkering gets you only so far. The endlessly shifting first draft becomes monumental, harder to question. The text defines its own reality, and you end up making only minimal changes – as if you were only its editor, rather than its author.

Sometimes, to make a breakthrough, you have to break away.

What I do is print out the first draft. (Which, as I've said, has already been edited and rewritten to some extent.) Reading it on paper, I mark any mistakes or anything I know I want to change. Often, if I'm dissatisfied or uncertain about something, I just put a wavy line or a question mark on the page to remind myself to think again. Although I work on-screen, I still find reading words on paper more comfortable. And it's surprising how many mistakes turn up on the page, even when I think I've done a careful on-screen editing job.

For the 'second draft,' I create a new document. That's right, I start all over again, on a blank screen-page, and I usually do this without referring to the first draft. Then – after a few paragraphs, or a few pages – I compare it to what I wrote the first time. I might decide that it was better the first time; usually I don't. If my first draft strikes me as particularly good in places, I copy-type for a while, but as soon as something strikes me as false or weak or wrong, I don't fiddle around trying to 'fix' it – I write something new.

Even if I'm copying directly from the manuscript, I use my PC like an old-fashioned typewriter for the revision. I resist the urge to 'import' any of my first-draft text out of its file into the current one. If what I've written is strong, it will stand up to being written again – either from memory, or copied off the page lying on the desk beside me. If it's weak, there's no way I'm going to go to the effort of retyping it – and as I haven't got the lazy option of letting it stand, I'm forced to try to do better. This works for me. Maybe it's not necessary for you, but give it a try – especially if you feel there's something wrong with what you've written, but can't quite work out what it is.

Structural revision

Starting all over again, as described above, is particularly helpful if your story needs major work. If you are happy that you've done what you intended, and it seems basically sound, then polishing and sharpening your language may be all that's needed.

But if your work needs a major rehaul, endlessly tinkering with the words on the screen simply prolongs the problem. Even shifting blocks of text around into different positions is not the solution.

Maybe you're not sure if your story needs major or minor work. Sometimes a trusted reader can help – not just anyone, and certainly not an adoring or uncritical friend. This is something that a writers' group or a good editor can help with. However, you may not have found the right (or any) writers' group, and professional editors don't have time to provide detailed criticisms or helpful suggestions for works they're not already committed to buying. Finally, you'll have to rely on yourself.

Even if you *do* have friends you trust to give a fair and critical reading, you'll need to be able to balance their comments against your own instincts.

Usually the best thing to do is to put the problematic manuscript aside for a few weeks or even months. Get on with writing something else. When you go back and re-read it after a break, you may be surprised at how different it seems. Instead of being blinded by what you *meant* to write, you should be able to read the story that you actually *wrote*. Flaws and weaknesses should be much more obvious once you've been away from the words for a while. Now that you can see the problems, you can start to think about the solutions.

Questions to ask yourself

Is there a problem with the point of view?

Would it be better if someone else told the story? The hero is not always the best viewpoint character – think how different the Sherlock Holmes stories would be if Holmes rather than Watson had narrated them. On the other hand, if your main character is too far removed from the action, you may miss out on the best scenes. If you're constantly relating interesting events at second-hand, reconsider your narrative point of view. Having multiple viewpoint characters is not advisable in a short story, but can open out a novel. Make sure that the viewpoint shifts are clearly signposted. Don't pop in and out abruptly, and don't use too many.

Is it the right length?

A novel needs a more complex plot and more characters; too many characters and complications can overburden a short story. Have you written any unnecessary scenes, or gone too far down blind alleys? Too many digressions, telling too much about minor characters, however interesting, can unbalance a story. Yet if you concentrate too single-mindedly on the plot, never wavering and never expanding, it may feel more like a very long synopsis than a novel. Does it go on for too long after the climax? Or does it end too soon, leaving the reader feeling up in the air and full of questions?

Is the basic premise interesting and believable?

If not, you might as well forget about rewriting, and start something new. Of course, there are no hard-and-fast rules about what is interesting – you can only go by your own feelings. Does the story you've told still interest *you*? If you bore yourself, you will certainly bore others. 'Believability' is another flexible term. Do your characters react plausibly? Can the reader sympathise with them? If this is science fiction, would your science convince a scientist? Can the ordinary reader follow your argument? Remember that although intellectually challenging SF is great, it should also be entertainment – not an IQ test.

Does it start in the right place?

Sometimes it is hard to be sure where the proper beginning of a story is until you've written it through to the end. Only when you're quite certain of the story you want to tell can you know if you've started too soon – before the important action begins – or too late, requiring a lot of flash-backs or expository lumps to explain who the characters are and how they came to be stranded on this alien planet or whatever. Flash-backs can be useful, but if a very long flash-back is required very near the beginning of a book, I tend to suspect that the author has started in the wrong place. (Unless it's part of a multi-book sequence, in which case some sort of filling-in to bring new readers up to speed may be necessary.)

Is the story well-constructed?

Every story will determine its own shape as well as its length, and much of that shape is down to pacing. 'Fast-paced' is usually a term of praise in fiction reviews, and often you can make improvements by speeding things up – avoiding scenes where nothing much happens, trimming away any material which doesn't immediately contribute to the main narrative flow. However, many admirable novels are deliberately slow-paced. If you want to instill a sense of wonder in your readers, or to let them live imaginatively in the world you've created, it would be foolish to race along at breakneck speed as if nothing mattered but the action. Most novelists vary the pace according to the needs of the story and the effect they want to achieve.

'Lean' novels and spare, stripped-down prose styles were once admired in genre fiction, but fashions have changed. These days, SF and fantasy novels are expected to be big, chunky books which will keep the reader absorbed in a detailed, fictional world for many days. The use of word-processors may be a contributing factor – it's so easy to keep adding material. Some books justify their length, but others would be improved by judicious trimming. Even when they are well-written and possess drama and interest in themselves, extraneous episodes can bog down a novel just as surely as the inclusion of too much unnecessary detail. Popular writers may be able to get away with going on a bit (especially about characters who've attracted a large following), but this is something the novice writer needs to think carefully about. Does the story you have to tell justify the time you've taken to tell it? Does every scene and subplot add to the interest, the richness, the excitement – or merely delay the obvious ending by another 20 pages? If the trek across the Dismal Desert was uneventful, you needn't devote more than a line to it – whether it took two weeks or two months. Perhaps you wrote 20 pages of hot, dusty days and spooky nights, with a little spurious suspense over whether or not the water supply would hold out. Rather than trying to beef up the suspense, or inventing more incidents, you might do better to cut the whole 20 pages. Unless something that happens in a scene is vital to the plot, or reveals something essential about the characters, you aren't obliged to describe it. Even though readers like to be involved, to feel they are living through events with the characters, they expect to be able to skip the boring bits. You don't have to detail every meal and rest-stop. As a writer you're not only free, but also practically obliged, to let time pass in a line-break, between chapters – and even, occasionally, to summarise: 'The trek across the Dismal Desert was no picnic, but it wasn't the nightmare the old man had painted it, either. Trudging along the rough road into Mahaar two weeks later, Kifi felt footsore, hungry and tired, but as determined as ever to confront her uncle with the truth.'

As well as irrelevant detail, 'loose ends' can contribute to a story's lack of shape. Although novels have more room for colourful details and detours than short stories do, digressions must be handled with care. Readers may feel cheated if they're introduced to a lot of characters who vanish, never to be heard from again, or if story-lines are left unfinished.

Foreshadowing, on the other hand, can add more power to a work of fiction. Foreshadowing is when an image or an incident, seemingly unimportant, takes on a greater significance as the story progresses. In my experience, foreshadowing is not entirely conscious – not in the first draft. It's at the rewriting stage that I discover which details have taken on an unexpected significance, which incidents need more description, and which ones need to be cut. Not by examining each one separately, but by seeing them in context, and deciding how – and whether – they fit into the whole story.

Does it deliver?

Every story sets up certain expectations in the reader, and must satisfy them – or be counted a failure. The only acceptable alternative to fulfilling the expectations you arouse is to *subvert* them: for example, what appears to be a traditional horror story might turn out to be humorous; or the reader's sympathy might be subtly transferred to the monster, so that the ending takes on a completely different meaning.

The ending should not be too easy; it should be felt to have been earned; and, whether happy, sad or ambiguous, it should feel like a proper conclusion.

Have you stopped too soon – are we left with too many unanswered questions and loose ends? Or have you gone on for too long after the climax, unable to leave your characters even though the drama has been played out?

Basic tools

I once heard an attendee at a writers' workshop contemptuously remark that he never bothered about spelling or grammar – that was an editor's job. I can't remember his name, but I'd be astonished if he ever made it into print.

Most manuscripts do get copy-edited, and corrected, before publication, and some copy-editors are extremely good and conscientious (despite being generally poorly paid) about their work. Other editors, rushed for time and strapped for cash, may assume that the author's mistakes are down to personal style, and leave them in. And all that is assuming that you've sold your manuscript in the first place.

These days, manuscripts full of misspellings and poorly constructed sentences look just as unprofessional as a novel written in purple ink on lined paper. They're hard to read, and they will not inspire an editor with confidence in your ability. If you can't spell and can't learn to spell, you should use a spell-check programme. Samuel R. Delany is one dyslexic author to whom word-processors have made a huge difference. However, it's worth bearing in mind that spell-checkers will not notice if a real word (like 'its' or 'discrete') is used in error for another real word (like 'it's' or 'discreet'), and it may also wrongly 'correct' words that it doesn't recognise (like proper names). For this reason you should always proof-read your manuscripts yourself (or get a friend to do it).

There may be computer programmes for checking your grammar, too – but I can't comment on how they work. Whenever I've chosen the 'check grammar' option on mine, all it does is query my irregular spacing.

There are those who do get riled up and write letters of protest to the BBC when supposedly once-sacrosanct rules of grammar are ignored. However, despite the unexpected popularity of Lynn Truss' 'zero tolerance' approach to grammar (*Eats, Shoots and Leaves*), most people – including writers and editors – feel that communication and clarity are the important things; they are the reason why the rules were formulated in the first place. If you don't feel confident about grammar and punctuation (or even if you do), buy a book or two about writing style. The one I had on my desk for 25 years is *The Elements of Style* by William Strunk, Jr. and E. B. White. Another good one is *The Reader Over Your Shoulder* by Robert Graves and Alan Hodge. The following is a bit of excellent advice from it:

> We suggest that whenever anyone sits down to write he should imagine a crowd of his prospective readers (rather than a grammarian in cap and gown) looking over his shoulder. They will be asking such questions as: 'What does this sentence mean?' 'Why do you trouble to tell me that again?' 'Why have you chosen such a ridiculous metaphor?' 'Must I really read this long, limping sentence?' 'Haven't you got your ideas muddled here?'

Saying what you mean to say and not confusing your readers – that's what's important. The common usage of punctuation and grammar is to aid understanding. If you're having a struggle with commas and semi-colons, or getting into a muddle with 'who' and 'whom', it might be a good idea to recast the whole sentence. Think of how you would say it to get across your meaning to someone else – and then write that down.

Which tense?

This is the past tense:

> The King was angry. He glared around the room, then snatched the crown from his own head and dashed it to the floor. 'Bring me the villain!' he shouted.

This is the present tense:

> The King is angry. He glares around the room. He snatches the crown from his own head and dashes it to the floor. 'Bring me the villain!' he shouts.

The past tense is normally used to write about events which have happened, and also about things which never happened – in other words, it's used to tell stories. Because stories contain their own past ('Years ago, no one had dared to contradict the King.'), their own present ('But now, he reflected bitterly, no one took him seriously. They were laughing at him!'), and speculations about the future ('When he found the traitor he would have his head cut off.'), the term 'past tense' can be a bit misleading. Ursula LeGuin suggests calling it the 'inclusive narrative tense'. This is the way in which nearly all the great fiction of the past and present has been written.

The present tense, which LeGuin calls the 'focused narrative tense', isn't able to embrace the continuity of past, present and future because it attempts to keep everything firmly in an artificial 'now'. During the past few decades, this technique has become more popular. Many writers who use it say they like its sense of 'immediacy' – yet, because it is actually a less natural way to tell a story, and can be awkward to handle consistently, its effect is actually to draw attention to itself and thus distance the reader from the story.

Focused narrative tense can be found in the works of any number of contemporary mainstream and literary writers, but is still relatively uncommon in SF and fantasy, especially at novel length. Two recent examples – both are literary (rather than genre) SF – are *The Time Traveller's Wife* by Audrey Niffenegger and *Oryx and Crake* by Margaret Atwood. Clearly, this is a stylistic choice, and it can be a useful tool, particularly for the writer wanting to move between different narrative strands. However, it should be handled with care. If it's used inconsistently, readers may be alienated.

Screenplays are written in the present indicative because, although they do tell a story, they exist to give directions about what is to happen on screen: 'King jumps up and down, howling. His crown bounces on the floor, and shatters. Cut away to servants cowering in terror.'

Editing to order

Often, when you've sold a short story or a novel, an editor will ask for some changes. These may be very minor (an editor tactfully pointing out your misuse of a word, or repetition of the same phrase three times in one paragraph), or they can be major, including changing the beginning or ending, adding or deleting subplots, or writing additional material. For the most part, these will be editorial *suggestions* – the editor thinks that the work would be improved if you made them; but if you disagree, you only have to say so. You should give all editorial suggestions serious consideration – editors are usually experienced and can bring an unprejudiced eye to a manuscript you may have been working on too long to see fresh. But editors aren't always right, and ultimately, it's your decision. There's no need to pick a fight about it; politely explain your reasons. The editor may even agree with you on reconsideration.

Occasionally, an editor will agree to buy a work on the understanding that the author will make certain changes to the manuscript before publication. If you won't, there's no sale. This is a straightforward decision: can you live with the revisions or would they ruin the book as you see it? After all, your name will be on it.

Sometimes, but rarely, an editor will ask for changes to be made before deciding whether or not to buy. This is a risky proposition, and it depends on what you're being asked to do. It will almost certainly involve a major rewrite. There is no guarantee that the editor will like what you've done; yet, if the suggested changes seem right to you, why not try it?

But do be sure that the editor really has asked to see it again. Sometimes an editor will try to be helpful by making suggestions about why your story was not successful. This might or might not be the reason why he or she didn't buy it, but it is *not* a request for revision. Unless an editor directly asks to see the manuscript again, don't send it back to them – even if you should decide to rework or rewrite it.

Letting go

Some writers don't know when to stop. Every time they re-read their manuscripts they can see something else they could improve. But there is a point at which it becomes only tinkering ... or worse. At some point, you must let it go, and send it out to the market. And keep sending it out until it is sold, or until you have run out of chances.

7
The Short Story

All novels are long stories, but a good short story is not a short novel. Short stories are more like poems, or, as Gwyneth Jones once suggested, good tunes, or riffs. They require a different approach from writing novels: different skills, challenges and rewards. Although much of what I've said about writing in the previous chapters applies to fiction of all lengths, I'm going to concentrate in this chapter on the short form, which has always had a special place at the very heart of science fiction and fantasy.

History

Genre SF evolved in the pages of American pulp magazines which, although they did serialise novels, devoted most of their pages to the novellas and short stories which seemed the ideal form for idea-driven SF. The 'weird tale' and classic fantasy had their own pulps, as did adventure stories, westerns, romances, and many other genres back in the days before television, DVDs and computers. The pulp magazines were practically extinct by the 1970s, but a few SF and fantasy fiction magazines struggled on and have survived into the present day. The market is small by earlier standards, and also by comparison with the sale of books; however, despite frequent gloomy predictions of its demise, the short story is not only alive but seems to have gained in popularity over the last couple of years. Following on from Booktrust's 'Save Our Short Story' campaign were several high-profile anthologies and competitions, and in September 2004, what was described as the 'first ever short-story festival' was held at Charleston in Sussex. Literary and mainstream short stories may receive more attention, but genre fiction, with its strong narrative drive, tends to be preferred by most readers, and SF, fantasy and horror are a part of the contemporary renaissance of the short story. Fantasy – at least, the bestselling contemporary variety – is unlike SF in being almost entirely novel-based. Words like 'epic' and 'saga', so often applied to popular fantasies, suggest a scale at odds with short fiction, and most readers turn to fantasy novels for their promise of a rich, detailed other-world in which they can live in imagination for days or weeks at a time. This is simply not a pleasure offered by the short story. However, the fantastic story does have a long and honourable pedigree, which includes the fairy tale, the ghost story, and much in between. There aren't many markets devoted specifically to short fantasy, but they turn up in many guises. The annual *Year's Best Fantasy and Horror* collections, edited by Ellen Datlow and Terri Windling, include lists of 'Honourable Mentions' and give a good idea of the scope and variety of the field.

Economics

Almost no one makes a living from writing short stories.

I was going to state, flatly, 'no one' – but there's always *someone*, boosted out of poverty by the legendary 'first-look' stipend from *The New Yorker*, or surviving on royalties, translations, film and TV options. Exceptions granted, the financially secure short-story writer must be a rarer beast than the bestselling poet.

There is a truism in publishing that 'short-story collections don't sell', and so they tend to be published, if at all, as part of a package deal (give us two novels and then we'll publish your short stories); as a means of attracting or keeping a desirable author; or as beautifully designed limited editions from small presses run more as a hobby than a business.

Most writers soon move from short stories to novels because of financial pressures, but there are good, practical reasons for writing short stories, especially at the beginning of your career.

A good training ground

At a time when fewer publishers will consider reading unsolicited manuscripts from unknown authors, and agents are even pickier about taking on untried clients, most SF and fantasy magazines are open to submissions from anyone. Internet sites, some of them now paying competitive rates, are eager for material. There are also many short-story competitions, most of which offer cash prizes and/or publication to new or previously published writers. A few of these originate within the genre, like the 'Writers of the Future' contest, but, while most do not, they may still be won by well-written, original SF or fantasy stories.

Despite their disinclination to publish short-story collections, most book editors keep an eye on what's happening in short fiction. Once you've had a few short stories published, you're a 'pro' – and that will give you an edge (how big a one depends on how good the stories are) in getting your novel considered by an agent or publisher.

Another 'plus' for the novice writer is that it's easier to get feedback on shorter work. Not only are editors more likely to explain where you went wrong, or why your story *almost* made the cut, but there are also non-paying markets for shorter material, and publication of any kind at least gives you the chance of having your work read. Creative writing classes and writers' groups both tend to favour short stories, which can be read and discussed as complete, finished works. Classes and groups which concentrate on novel-writing are much rarer, and require the novelist to share the work-in-progress before it's finished – a risky proposition. Reading and criticising a novel in pieces isn't always very helpful. Larger structural or thematic problems may be missed, and small problems can get blown out of proportion. Negative criticism at an early stage can fatally erode the author's confidence; it is easier to bounce back from the savaging of a ten-page story than from the discovery that nobody likes the first 100 pages of your novel. Short stories can be discussed and criticised not only on a line-by-line basis, but also as a whole: does the plot make sense? Are the characters believable? Does the ending feel right?

The short story is less daunting for a beginner because it is not as complex as a novel, and not so demanding of your time. Stories can be held in your head, worked out while doing dishes or stocking shelves, and written completely in one to half-a-dozen sittings. Novels can take years to write, especially if you have to fit the writing in with a full-time job and other commitments; but if you can't manage to finish a short story in your spare time, you might as well give up.

The importance of *practice* can't be over-emphasised. Writers write; that's what distinguishes them from daydreamers fantasising about celebrity. The only way to become a better writer is to do it – not to theorise, or tell people your ideas, or read books about how to do it, but to sit down to write (every day if possible), and finish what you write. Short stories, whether or not they're ever published, are a great place to practise and learn basic skills. Whereas the novel-in-progress can, like analysis, go on and on interminably, short stories have an obviously attainable end.

The writer, editor and publisher Peter Crowther says that writers who don't 'hone their craft and practise their plotting and dialogue techniques in the short form' *before* writing their first novel are 'wasting everyone's time'. I don't entirely agree. Being able to write a decent short story does not guarantee that you can write a novel; conversely, there are some very fine novelists who simply don't see the *point* of a short story, and who've learned and honed their skills in other ways.

Having said that, I must confess that my own career followed the very path Peter recommends. As a place to begin your career as a writer, the short story can't be bettered.

Awards

When literary awards are mentioned, people tend to think of the Man Booker Prize, or the Whitbread or the National Book Award – all for book-length works. Short stories don't attract the same attention – except within the SF and fantasy field.

The Hugo – also known as the Science Fiction Achievement Award – voted on by members of the World Science Fiction Convention, is awarded annually to the best novel, novella, novelette, and short story. The Nebula, presented by the Science Fiction and Fantasy Writers of America (SFFWA), also recognises the same four categories. The Tiptree Award, given to 'the work of fantasy or science fiction which best expands and explores the concept of gender', may be awarded to a short story *or* a novel, at the discretion of the judges. World Fantasy Awards are handed out to novels and to short fiction, and also for the best anthology or collection of short stories published in a given year. The British Fantasy Award is given annually for a novel and a short story.

The John W. Campbell Award exists to recognise new writers, and has been won by writers (including me, back in 1973) who've had only a few short stories published.

As you may gather from the above, it is possible to become critically acclaimed as an SF writer without publishing a novel. Harlan Ellison and Howard Waldrop are two well-known, highly praised writers whose reputations depend almost entirely upon their short stories. Although she began writing novels relatively late in life, Carol Emshwiller was known long before then for the blazing originality of her quirky short stories. Theodore Sturgeon, Ray Bradbury, Robert Sheckley and Joanna Russ have all written full-length books, but they made their first, most powerful impact with highly memorable short stories.

How long?

For purposes of the major awards – and, therefore, most markets – the short story is defined as a work of fiction under 7,500 words; the novelette from 7,500 to 17,500 words; and the novella from 17,500 to 40,000 words. Anything over 40,000 words is therefore a novel. However, these days most publishers would consider an SF novel under 60,000 words as 'too short' for publication unless it was aimed at children, and the average fantasy novel is usually well over 100,000 words.

Many competitions, and a few markets, impose very strict word-limits – sometimes short stories must be kept under 3,000 words. Stories under 1,000 words are called 'short-shorts'. Outside the SF field there is little scope for the publication of anything in-between the novel and the short story. However, the long short story ('novelette') and the short novel ('novella') are regularly published and admired by SF fans. So don't despair if your story falls in-between the 'ideal' lengths for the short story and the novel.

Writing in *The New York Review of Science Fiction* in November 2000, Darrell Schweitzer began with 'two premises: 1) the novella is in many ways the best form for science fiction, and 2) the novella is the hardest to sell professionally'. The regular magazines don't have space to publish more than half-a-dozen novellas in a given year, and book publishers are reluctant to risk a shorter-than-average novel. Hence, Schweitzer offered his third premise, that 'the small press flows in like water to fill whatever gaps the monoliths of major New York publishing leave open' and argued that by concentrating on this gap in the market, small presses offered both writers and readers best value. Here in Britain, PS Publishing has established a wide-ranging, highly regarded list of novellas published in signed, limited editions.

Stories should dictate their own length, but it is wise to aim to keep your story as short and tightly written as possible. While 'loose, baggy monsters' of novels may expand, like magical carpet-bags, to include all sorts of additional matter, subplots and fascinating digressions, the successful short story is nearly always neat, trim and to the point. It must project one single vision and be tightly focused throughout, every detail a necessary, telling one. The best short stories are like poems, with every word essential.

Competition word-limits may seem frustratingly arbitrary, but trying to fit the story you have to tell into a restricted space is a useful exercise. It can highlight what's important about the story, and teach you different means of expression. SF stories, in particular, can be too complex, requiring too much explanation or background detail to be really successful at the shortest lengths; however, for some effects, the very short story is ideal, delivering an undiluted punch.

Some writers seem incapable of 'writing short'. Sometimes a story can't be told in under 10,000 words, it's true; but sometimes, paradoxically, length is a sign of uncertainty or laziness, revealing the writer's footsteps as he or she pads uncertainly around the main point, gradually creeping up on it. Word-limits force you to concentrate and find the most vivid and efficient way of expressing yourself. Even when there's nothing obviously *wrong* with the writing, sometimes cutting a few hundred words will transform a rather ordinary tale into something much sharper and more memorable. Here are some suggestions for how to prune:

- Cut the adjectives and make the verbs work harder. Trim long passages of 'realistic' dialogue to a crisp, informative exchange, or summarise what was said. Is that long survey of the surroundings really necessary? Hints, impressions and one perfect single detail can convey an atmosphere more powerfully than pages of description.
- Be concise. Explain less. Dramatise important scenes, but remember that despite the usual advice given to writers, on occasion, to keep the narrative flowing, information may be 'told' instead of 'shown'.
- Be ruthless. Cutting a paragraph isn't like chopping off a limb. You're allowed to change your mind. As long as you don't destroy earlier drafts, you can always put everything back as it was.

If some writers suffer from the need to tell too much, others get stuck at 3,000 or so words and can't see how to move on. These days, I tend to write mostly novellas and novels, but at the start of my career, 1,000–3,000 words was my favoured length. All the ideas I had for stories could be adequately explored within ten typed pages; much more, it seemed to me, would be padding. This tendency was doubtless reinforced by my experience as a newspaper journalist and a preference for writing a complete work at one single long sitting.

And then one day I was asked to write a novelette. The minimum I could get away with was 8,000 words, and my editor told me he'd prefer at least 12,000 words. I was used to writing short stories from a single viewpoint, with action that took place over the course of a few days. For the new story – which became 'The Family Monkey' – I therefore decided to use multiple viewpoints and a time-span of several decades. *No way* could I fit all that into 3,000 words!

As I described in Chapter 2, the idea for 'The Family Monkey' came from a supposedly true event I'd read about: that a mysterious airship had crashed in West Texas in 1897; that an alien, inhuman body had been recovered from the wreckage and buried in the local graveyard. That could have made a nice, succinct short story ... I could imagine writing about the effect of witnessing this crash on an old-time Texas rancher ... but what if the alien had survived the crash? What would happen next? I was intrigued by the notion of a 'close encounter' on the frontier, and setting several different characters in conflict with this one, damaged, alien intelligence offered me a lot of scope. In fact, what I had was almost a novel in miniature. In retrospect, I think that it is a bit too short – the ending, in particular, feels rushed and is distinctly underwritten – but writing it was a very useful learning experience.

Multiple viewpoints and action taking place over longer periods of time are obvious ways of opening out a story, but they are far from the only ones. An exotic background, multiple characters, more plot, more complex issues at stake ... all these require more depth, and therefore more wordage, than two characters in conflict against a well-worn setting. The length of the story depends on what you want to say, and the impression you want to create. Many writers find that ideas seem to come marked with a pre-set, obvious length, while others discover how long a story needs to be by writing it.

Types of stories

Some types of fictional narrative are better suited to short stories than to novels.

Ghost stories

Although some writers – Shirley Jackson, Peter Straub, Dan Simmons, Jonathan Aycliffe and Susan Hill come to mind – have managed to sustain the fear and tension of the ghost story at book length, the best, classic ghost stories are shorter. *The Turn of the Screw* by Henry James is one of the best; others who have written classics in the field include M. R. James, Robert Aickman, Edith Wharton and Elizabeth Bowen. Ghosts are ambiguous; if you see them too clearly, they stop being scary and may even seem a bit ridiculous. To write about something as insubstantial as a ghost, keeping the vague threat just on the edge of being seen or explained away, is a difficult balancing act, but can be perfectly achieved in a short story.

One-punch stories

These are constructed rather like jokes, and stand or fall on the strength of the 'punch-line' – the final (and meant to be unexpected) revelation at the end. If over-long, they become tedious; there's also the risk that the reader will figure out where you're going. When good, these are memorable and much in demand; most, sadly, are not very good.

Depressing stories

As I said in an earlier chapter, editors and readers tend to prefer 'upbeat' endings, and the most popular novels provide them. 'Miserabilist' fictions which take a relentlessly grim view of the world and human nature and end badly are more acceptable in shorter forms, perhaps because the reader has invested less time in getting to know and care about the characters. A tragic or depressing story, well-told, may be all the more effective for being brief. My first collection of short stories, *A Nest of Nightmares*, was published with the cover shout-line, 'Into the

119

worlds of loneliness, anxiety and fear.' It was appropriate, all right, but hardly an attractive lure to a mass-market readership; no wonder it was never reprinted!

'Plotless' stories

A novel without a plot is hardly a novel at all, yet many modern short stories happily do without. They may be described as mood-pieces, or a slice of life. They can be a display of style, an experiment with language, or a psychological study.

For Edgar Allan Poe, the purpose of a short story was to evoke one particular emotional atmosphere. Some fantasy and horror stories operate on this level, aiming to arouse a particular emotional response in the reader – awe, wonder, terror, or fear. The situation may be far-fetched or even inexplicable, as in Poe or Kafka, concentrating on exploring the mental and psychological state of the main character.

Although science fiction tends to be plot-driven, it doesn't have to be. In Howard Waldrop's novelette 'You *Could* Go Home Again', for example, almost nothing happens: the story opens with a departure from Japan after the Tokyo Olympics of 1940; Fats Waller gives a musical performance for his fellow passengers, while Thomas Wolfe, on his way home, drifts in and out of earshot. The story ends without conflict or resolution, which would normally be seen as a complete 'no-no' for the genre writer – yet this is undeniably first-rate science fiction. The point of his (extremely accomplished) story is to make the background real and comprehensible to the reader, to bring an alternative reality to life, and Waldrop does it beautifully.

Experimental fiction

It's still possible to take risks in the short form which would be labelled 'unpublishable' if attempted at book-length. But it is worth pointing out that the *successful* experiment is even more difficult to write than the old-fashioned, traditionally plotted story – and also that the lack of an obvious plot-line does not mean a story is unstructured. In an autobiographical piece, Carol Emshwiller commented: 'A lot of people don't seem to understand how planned and plotted even the most experimental of my stories are. I'm not interested in stories where anything can happen at any time. I set up clues to foreshadow what will happen and what is foreshadowed does happen. I try to have all, or most, of the elements in the stories, linked to each other ... How I write is by linking and by structures, and by, I hope, not ever losing sight of the meaning of the story.'

Parodies

Book-length parodies of popular works are seldom wholly successful, but this type of humorous writing can be very enjoyable at shorter lengths. John Sladek wrote a brilliant series of stories parodying the style and concerns of popular SF writers; Joseph F. Pumilia created a sub-Lovecraftian writer by the name of M. M. Moamrath for some humorous horror fantasies. Related to the parody is *pastiche*, in which another, admired writer's style is deliberately adopted; for example, 'Tom Sawyer's Sub-Orbital Escapade', which I wrote in collaboration with Steven Utley. Non-fiction forms like newspaper articles, book reviews and scientific reports can be another way of telling a story, not necessarily for humorous effect.

Brilliant ideas

Original ideas have novelty value, and are highly prized in science fiction, so that occasionally an editor will overlook poor writing and buy an otherwise mediocre story for its 'great idea'. Many early SF stories were a means of presenting – hardly exploring – new concepts, but these stories are read only as curiosities today. Modern readers expect not only original ideas, but also a good, involving story told in clear prose. In the long run, the originality of an idea matters less than what is done with it. It is also worth bearing in mind that just because *you've* never run across a particular notion in fiction before doesn't mean it hasn't been used. Although it is still possible to sell a story on the strength of a really good idea, this is no way to build a career. The best writers always go a bit further, developing the idea, personalising it, and pushing the boundaries.

'Real' short stories

These are pure gold, always in demand by editors and readers alike. An exciting, original story with plot and characters, well-written and classically structured, not complex enough to be a novel, but precisely as long as it needs to be.

Hard work

Short stories take less actual writing time than novels, but that doesn't mean they are the easier option. A lot of thinking and planning can go into each one, even if much of the work is unconscious.

Roald Dahl, famous for his children's books, began by writing short stories for adults. Many are macabre, sometimes with elements of the supernatural, and all are what he called 'real' short stories – that is, carefully plotted, and often with a sting in the tail. In an interview many years ago, Dahl told me that they were 'the result of 25 years of solid work, doing nothing else, absolutely nothing but these short stories'. After producing three volumes' worth of them, he ran out of ideas. It was his opinion that 'finding plots' was hard work, and that there was only a limited number of good ones available to any author.

The fix-up

This is a book category which seems almost unique to science fiction, and refers to novels constructed out of previously published short stories – usually with the addition of some specially written new material. Many SF and fantasy writers, having created a particular background for one story, find themselves drawn back to it again and again until they've written enough short stories to fill a book. Sometimes, especially when the same characters reappear, the collection may feel like an episodic novel. This multi-story technique also works for a panoramic novel covering a vast sweep of time – in much SF and fantasy, the background has the function of a character. Examples of short stories linked together to form a novel include *Orphans of the Sky* by Robert Heinlein and *A Canticle for Leibowitz* by Walter M. Miller.

Something similar is the collection of short stories which share thematic concerns, published and described as a novel – like *The Martian Chronicles* by Ray Bradbury or *The Seedling Stars* by James Blish. However, this designation has to do with marketing concerns – novels sell better than short-story collections – and editors today are as reluctant to buy a collection of 'linked' stories as they are about the usual kind.

Avoiding clichés

Every cliché was new once, and it's a sad fact that most of the hackneyed old ideas that turn up in the stories which editors reject immediately have come from writers who honestly think they're absolutely original.

There are a number of reasons why writers hit this stumbling block even when they've achieved some ability to write reasonably well.

Ignorance
The writer has read little or no SF but has had a 'brilliant idea'. The only cure for this is to read, read, read – not only recently published works, but the classics in the field too. Notice how similar ideas have been used in different ways over the years.

The surprise ending
The last man and woman on earth are called Adam and Eve. God is a bored child. The big battle for the fate of the universe is actually a computer game played by aliens. The mysterious, newly discovered planet is really our own abandoned earth. The hero has gone back in time and become his own father. It was all a dream. What can I tell you? Editors really have read it all before. If the whole point of a story is to astonish the reader,

you've got to have a genuinely weird and wonderful mind to do that – and even then you'll be lucky if you manage to write a dozen effective one-punch stories. To avoid failure, forget the 'surprise'. Try pushing beyond the ending. Write about something more personal. Explore the possibilities of different types of stories, where the impact is not all loaded into the last few lines.

The easy option

The writer has fallen back on stock characters and/or situations: the mad scientist, the deadly female assassin, the godlike computer, the cuddly alien. They are the first things to come to mind, and they are second-hand at best. Novelists have more room to develop their characters and backgrounds slowly, through the accretion of incident and detail. Characters in short stories need just as much thought and work as characters in novels if they are to be believable, but all that work has to be done off the page. Test your writing against your own feelings and experiences. Ask yourself how you would behave in the same situation. Give your hero or heroine a few weaknesses, and some friends as well as his or her major conflict, and consider the complications of real life. Be observant of how real people talk and act, and don't always go with your first impulse. Rewrite.

Marketing your stories

When you've written a story, and worked on it and rewritten it until you feel it is the very best you can do, it's time to find a home for it. Since editors have never conducted door-to-door searches for good material, you'll have to go to them. Although I think that deliberate attempts to write 'to' a particular market tend to lead to derivative hackwork and failure, you should familiarise yourself with what's currently being published.

Reading annual 'best of the year' anthologies will make you aware of the level of competition, and their acknowledgements pages can help you track down little magazines and small presses. Joining SF and fantasy organisations and on-line discussion groups will also give you access to market information. (See Chapter 9 for more details.) It's always advisable to read issues of a magazine before submitting stories to them, and to follow any guidelines they offer. These are often available on the Internet as well.

What do editors want?

I asked several prominent editors in the field to help me here. My questions are followed by their answers, below.

What sort of stories are you looking for?

Gordon Van Gelder has worked as an editor in the field since 1988, and is the editor and publisher of *The Magazine of Fantasy and Science Fiction*. He replied:

'Short answer: science fiction.

Longer answer: intellectually challenging stories of science fiction (preferably) or fantasy with well-developed characters.

Longest answer: Ed Ferman [former editor and publisher] told me that since the 1950s we've always received more good fantasy than we could possibly publish and never enough science fiction. In recent years, I've found this is growing *more* true. It seems like fewer writers are actually writing science fiction and more writers are lazily letting Arthur C. Clarke's dictum that "any sufficiently advanced technology is indistinguishable from magic" serve as a licence for them not to think through the speculative elements of their stories. The results are a lot of "soft" SF stories that are so soft they squish – and I find myself looking harder for well-told stories with any real scientific content to them. That's the sort of stories I'd most like to find right now.'

Sheila Williams, a professional editor for more than 22 years, took the helm as editor of *Isaac Asimov's Science Fiction Magazine* in 2004. She replied:

'My own editorial tastes are not wildly divergent from those of the previous editor, Gardner Dozois. I enjoy intelligent, well-written science fiction with strong and believable characters and innovative ideas. I have a preference for hard science fiction, but don't plan to fill the magazine up solely with that sort of story. Isaac himself wrote fantasy for *Asimov's* (the then-editor made him change his demon into an alien, but he changed it right back for book publication), and the magazine has a heritage of running some very fine fantasies over the years. We've also run a lot of different kinds of science-fiction stories in the magazine, and I intend to continue this tradition.'

Ellen Datlow, an award-winning anthologist and short-story editor for nearly 25 years, replied from her position as fiction editor for www.scifi.com:

'I need more SF than fantasy. I'd love literate, intelligent, well-characterised hard SF – but who wouldn't? I take some urban fantasy, but I'm not wild about historical fantasy.'

Are there any types of stories, or subjects, that you wish you'd never see again?

Gordon Van Gelder:

'The short answer is no, because the minute I say "I never want to see another story about sentient pizzas" (or whatever), I'll receive just such a story that knocks me out.

'But I can say that I've never been much of an enthusiast for elf stories, and in the last three or four years (particularly since 9 September 2001) I've seen so many stories about zombies and the dead returning that I'd gladly go a year without reading another one.

'Lately I've noticed another type of story that doesn't do much for me anymore. In the same way that poets and critics dubbed stories that romanticise the landscape as "the pathetic fallacy", I call them the "Disney fallacy" stories: these are contemporary fantasy stories, almost invariably with one element of magic, and the magic works to bring about redemption or salvation for the character solely because she/he is such a good person deep down that, by golly, magic *ought* to work for him or her. A lot of Disney films use this formula, and it's potent, but it's also overworked and I've found that for a story of this sort to convince me, it needs some sort of a different spin to it.'

Sheila Williams:

'Although it's tempting to do so, it's always dangerous to make such a pronouncement. Say, "I don't want to see any more ... World Trade Center stories," and I'd miss out on Lucius Shepard's "Only Partly Here"; ... clone stories, and I'd miss out on L. Timmel Duchamp's "How Josiah Taylor Lost His Soul"; ... high fantasy, and I'd miss out on some of Michael Swanwick's best work. To be successful, though, all ideas have to be looked at from a refreshing new angle – but it's generally safe to keep in mind that I don't usually care for high fantasy.'

Ellen Datlow:

'I've seen too many stories about dying, death and ghosts, and too many alternative histories.'

What are some of the most common mistakes made by novice SF or fantasy writers?

Gordon Van Gelder:

'Several common mistakes are:

- Not grounding the story in the opening. It shouldn't take seven pages for me to figure out where the story is set or what the characters are like.
- Not developing the setting. I don't need 50 pages of background research, but beginners frequently operate

on the assumption that a story without a definite locale will feel universal. Instead, such a story has a generic feel that works against it.

- Central casting. I see a lot of stories in which the characters are familiar types; so familiar that I find I don't care about them.'

Sheila Williams:

- 'Stories are often underpopulated. There is just the one main character who interacts with extremely clichéd characters, if he or she interacts with anyone else at all.
- Stories begin in a boring way because the character is living in a boring situation (to be jazzed up later by some exciting adventure). This tedious beginning should be avoided at all costs.
- Many viewpoint characters are completely unlikable (obviously heading toward some just dessert) and that makes it very hard for the reader to care enough to continue reading.
- Young authors often base characters entirely on themselves, with no thought given to the characterisation and motivations of other sorts of people (e.g. children, parents, middle-aged and older people).'

Ellen Datlow:

- 'They think they're doing something new when they aren't.
- They don't create and develop an interesting story with characters who draw the reader in.
- Poor use of language.'

What advice would you give to aspiring SF and fantasy writers?

Gordon Van Gelder:

'All the general advice that has been around since Robert A. Heinlein was a lad still applies. I'll add that in the

Internet age there are more opportunities than ever to get feedback on your story before you submit it – either from online workshops or from correspondents. When you submit a story for publication it should be a polished version, not a first draft.

'I also tell would-be writers not to defeat themselves. When you're writing fiction, you're laying yourself out there for everyone to see, so of course you're as vulnerable as a nude model ... but be professional, be persistent, and don't take any of it personally. I hear anecdotes all the time about promising writers who defeat themselves because they overreact to one well-intended comment, or who send editors five pages of rebuttals every time they receive a rejection letter.'

Sheila Williams:
'Try not to make any of the mistakes mentioned above. Don't be imitative – get inspirations from cultures that haven't already been thoroughly mined for fantasy; read popular science magazines for the latest breakthroughs in science.'

Ellen Datlow:
'Read some of the classics to get a feeling for the field; read widely outside the field, and be willing to experiment with style, tone and voice.'

Would you care to hazard any predictions about the future of science fiction and/or fantasy as a genre?

Gordon Van Gelder:
'I think the fantasy field will continue to prosper. The Young Adult fantasy field has over-expanded in the wake of *Harry Potter*, and I wonder if that particular area will contract in the next couple of years. I worry about the future of science fiction, as noted above, but I continue to believe the future will be better, and every time I open an envelope I think the story enclosed will knock my socks off.'

Sheila Willliams:

'Judging from the credentials many people list on their submissions, the SF and fantasy markets seem pretty healthy. At least, there are a lot of online and semi-professional print magazines that will publish a beginner's work. While the quality of these outlets varies, they do provide new authors with a place to hone their craft. The number of outlets seems to imply that there are a lot of people interested in reading this material. I hope that the fanzines, the online zines, and the professional magazines like *Asimov's* can continue to find these readers. The field is constantly refreshed by exciting new work and new authors. I'm glad *Asimov's* is around to encourage that work. The professional science fiction magazine is still the first place most professional authors break into. We're still the first paying market willing to take a risk on a new author. We have to, because we lose so many of our writers to novel-writing! Fortunately, some major novelists, viz. Walter Jon Williams, Connie Willis, Joe Haldeman, Ursula K. LeGuin, etc., continue to write short fiction, too.'

Ellen Datlow:

'Ha! I wouldn't dare predict! However ... I do feel if the digest-sized magazines don't change in some way they'll be gone within ten years. They really *are* invisible on the newsstands, and that's where and how you attract new readers.'

8
Writing for Children

The very best children's fantasy can be read with pleasure by adults as well as by children. This has always been true, although the unprecedented success of the *Harry Potter* series has somewhat obscured the fact that classics like *Alice's Adventures in Wonderland*, *The Wind in the Willows*, *Peter Pan* and *The Hobbit*, not to mention traditional folk and fairy tales, have always been enjoyed by readers of all ages.

Before fantasy became the marketable, highly commercial genre it is today, it was often seen as suitable only for children. Charles Perrault's fairy tales, originally written to amuse the courtiers of 17th-century France, and Jonathan Swift's satirical *Gulliver's Travels* (although abridged and bowdlerised) were moved into the children's section, and when J.R.R. Tolkien, Alan Garner, Ursula LeGuin and others wrote novels set in other worlds, they were originally published as children's fiction.

Although *Harry Potter and the Philosopher's Stone* appeared on Bloomsbury's children's list in 1997, the book's growing fame meant that it was later issued in two different paperback editions: one had a more grown-up-looking cover illustration (and higher price tag) for the benefit of anyone who felt uncomfortable being seen reading a book obviously meant for children.

The success of the *Harry Potter* series has transformed the whole business of publishing books for children, and fantasy has remained at the forefront of the ongoing boom. However, whether this is the dawning of a new 'golden age' in children's literature, or a disastrous over-expansion, remains to be seen.

Why write for children?

Thirty years ago, if you had an idea for a fantasy novel, your best bet for getting published was to aim it at younger readers because that was where fantasy 'belonged'. Although the marketing situation is very different now, there are still certain types of fantasy which do seem more suitable for children than adults, just as there are some writers who prefer to write for children. Many of the most popular fantasy writers have said that they do not consciously aim at a particular age-group.

In an article first published in 1968, Alan Garner declared, 'I do not write for children, but entirely for myself. Yet I do write for some children, and have done so from the beginning.' He went on to explain: 'Only recently have I come to realise that, when writing for myself, I am still writing for children; or, rather, for adolescents. By adolescence I mean an arbitrary age of somewhere between ten and 18. This group of people is the most important of all, and it makes the best audience. Few adults read with a comparable involvement.'*

In an interview for *Newsweek*, J. K. Rowling said of *Harry Potter and the Philosopher's Stone*: 'I wasn't really aware that it was a children's book. I really wrote it for me. It was what I found funny and what I liked.'

G. P. Taylor, author of *Shadowmancer* and *Wormwood*, has acknowledged that it was the popularity of books such as Philip Pullman's *His Dark Materials* and the *Harry Potter* series which made him determined to write fantasy with a strong Christian message. However, he told an interviewer, 'I wrote for any age-group. My books are read by more adults than children. I just wrote the books; I didn't intend them for children or adults, I just wrote a book.'

Some writers may be particularly attuned to children's interests through their experience as teachers, social workers or parents, with an ability to think on their wave-length and anticipate their interests. But I suspect that most of the best writers

*from *The Voice that Thunders*

for children identify imaginatively more with children than with their fellow adults because they remember their own childhoods so strongly and perhaps, in a way, never entirely grew up.

More than a decade ago, Diana Wynne Jones, an extremely accomplished and popular author of children's fiction, decided to try her hand at writing for adults, imagining that it would give her more freedom. Later she said she'd found the opposite to be true: editors imposed more rules and restrictions because adult readers had fixed expectations of what 'should' happen in a fantasy, whereas children were more open-minded, and wouldn't baulk at crossing genre borders.

I was interested to hear Darren Nash, senior editor of Atom, Time Warner UK's Young Adult SF and fantasy list, echo this sentiment when he said, 'There's a freedom available in young adult writing that's not always available in an adult list. There, if a writer does something a bit different, it may get good reviews but not sell all that well, while the latest epic commercial fantasy is selling in huge quantities. The teen market seems more receptive to people doing things that are a bit different. My personal belief is that growing up is all about learning to compartmentalise. That's what adults do; we say "this belongs in the fantasy box, but this is SF, so that goes in a different box" and we don't like things from one box turning up in the other. Whereas for kids, everything is new, they don't have fixed expectations, and if things are wonderful and interesting they can all fit into the same book.'

The best reason for writing for children is if you feel that the story you want to tell, or the issues that interest you, might strike an especially strong chord in younger readers. It should never be considered the easier option, or as 'practice' for the 'grown-up' books you intend to write later.

How children's fantasy is different

Most fantasies written for children have children as main characters. But while having a young adult as the protagonist will make a novel more appealing to young readers, it doesn't necessarily make it a children's book. (Consider *Lord of the Flies*.)

Certain subjects and themes – for example, growing up or leaving home – predominate in many works for young adults. The entry on children's fantasy in *The Encyclopedia of Fantasy* suggests that the theme of transformation is a key element in distinguishing children's from adult fantasy: 'The ability to experience either a transfer of self from place to place or through time, or a change in being (from poverty to riches or from beast to beauty). The latter process is particularly important as it allows the child to come to terms with its own change from child to adult.'

Some types of fantasies, even when they are read by increasing numbers of adults, may be more acceptable when they're categorised as being for children. The sub-genre dubbed 'secret garden' fantasies by *The Encyclopedia of Fantasy*, for example, is one in which our world is shown to contain another, hidden world into which the protagonist can escape from time to time. Although the secondary-world fantasy has become relatively respectable adult fare, perhaps the secret garden is best viewed through childish eyes. Grown-ups, in children's books, can be useless, unobservant and dim-witted to a degree which would raise howls of disbelief from adults reading an adult novel.

Children's fantasies offer an imaginative freedom to the author who can shrug off the burden of adult self-consciousness and see the world with fresh vision. But there are also some limitations.

Taboos

Few subjects are absolutely forbidden in children's books these days, but sex, death, violence and religious beliefs must be handled with great care if they are to be acceptable. Bad language – having characters swearing realistically – is guaranteed to cause trouble with librarians and teachers. Plot-turns which have children befriended by or reliant upon adult strangers used to be a commonplace in popular fiction but are a danger area today. Children's writers have to be careful not to suggest activities which could get real children into trouble. Fortunately, the removed-from-everyday-reality settings of most fantasy allow more freedom than does the 'realistic' novel.

Too much emphasis on any explicitly adult concern – whether romantic love, finances, child-rearing, politics or any other grown-up business – certainly won't appeal to young readers. If these are vital to your story, perhaps it's not really appropriate for children.

Young adults

This category, often abridged to YA, developed in the 1960s and remains difficult to define precisely – sitting somewhat uneasily between children's and adult fiction. The core audience is teenagers, but these days publishers can reasonably hope that particularly strong and unusual books, like Mark Haddon's *The Curious Incident of the Dog in the Night-Time* or Meg Rosoff's *How I Live Now*, will break out of the age-ghetto and attract a large adult readership as well.

The main character of a YA novel is usually a teenager, although some are adult narrators recalling events long in the past, as in Rachel Klein's eerie *The Moth Diaries*. The writing style may be simple or sophisticated, 'easy' or 'difficult', even poetic and experimental. Apart from avoiding obscenities (the teens won't be shocked, but their parents and teachers might make a fuss) there's no need to make any concessions in style or language. Subjects best avoided in fiction for younger children, including sex, drug-use, violence and death, can be tackled head-on. Honesty is highly regarded. Attempts to 'write down' to or lecture your readers will alienate them.

YA lists come and go and are redesigned, trying to attract this constantly changing readership. Publishers and booksellers have told me that this age-group is the hardest to reach. It is also the hardest to define, with the same books appearing at different times on either adult or YA lists, depending on shifts in the market or editorial whim. Librarians usually shelve YA titles separately from the rest of the children's fiction to keep younger readers from being exposed to inappropriate material. I noticed that Philip Pullman's books were shelved in the children's section of my local library until the librarian read *The Subtle Knife* for herself, at which point she moved all three volumes of *His Dark Materials* into YA. There's no doubt that some children might be disturbed by this very powerful work; it's fierce, scary and uncompromising.

Harry Potter and the Philosopher's Stone is definitely a children's book. However, as the series has progressed, and Harry has grown into a teenager, the books increased in length and complexity – and so has J. K. Rowling's prose style. *Harry Potter and the Goblet of Fire* and *Harry Potter and the Order of the Phoenix* are probably more accurately classified as Young Adult fantasies, although their appeal is certainly not limited to that age-group. In 2001, *Harry Potter and the Goblet of Fire* won the 'Best Novel' Hugo – an award never before given to a children's book.

Younger readers

So far, I've been discussing books for readers over the age of about nine. Although picture books are outside the scope of this book, there are plenty of titles aimed at beginner and 'newly independent' readers. Children's reading skills can't be absolutely defined by their age, but generally the group that publishers consider to be 'younger readers' are under the age of nine or ten.

Books for younger readers are shorter (usually between 3,000 and 12,000 words), have plenty of illustrations (books for beginner readers 'support the text' with a picture on every page), and favour a simple, basic vocabulary. Most publishers have lists targeted at a particular age or reading ability. Educational reading schemes tend to be structured around core vocabularies, with authors briefed on the expected style or format, but in general publishing there's usually more flexibility and freedom for the author.

At this age-level there's no division into genres. Some lists prefer plots to be based around family, school and friends or animals, but fantasy, especially when it is light and humorous, is usually welcome. Fantasy characters like Tony Bradman's 'Dilly the Dinosaur' are popular, and elements of science fiction, like space ships, aliens and monsters, are often seen as a good way of getting boys interested in reading.

One small book

My first book for younger readers was *Mad House*. I'd written a couple of YA novels for one publisher when I was commissioned to write something for the 'Mammoth Reads' list, defined as being for 'children who are growing in reading confidence and looking for a more substantial read'. I was told it should be 8,000 words long and divided into four or five chapters.

Although 8,000 words is the length of a short story, *Mad House* had to be approached and structured like a miniature novel. That, for me, was the biggest challenge. I knew I could write an 80,000-word novel, or an 8,000-word short story – but could I write an 8,000-word novel?

The basic idea for the book came from a newspaper article about a 'smart fridge' which would automatically order groceries whenever you started to run low. Since I believe that everything designed to solve one problem invariably creates others, I felt certain this wouldn't work, and brooded on the many ways it might go wrong. I'd read and seen too much science fiction on the theme of the mad computer to think my ideas were especially original: Harlan Ellison's bleak, brilliant short story 'I Have No Mouth and I Must Scream', Dean Koontz's early SF novel *Demon Seed*, and of course the computer HAL in Stanley Kubrick/Arthur C. Clarke's *2001: A Space Odyssey* all jostled together in my mind.

But as I realised that my audience would not be a bunch of

jaded old SF fans, but rather young readers to whom the idea of a computer-run 'smart house' might be new, I came to see that I did have a story worth telling. Envisioning it from a child's point of view made an old idea new. The word-limit made it a challenge. The format and audience determined the kind of story it had to be.

All the mad-computer stories I thought of were downbeat, even tragic tales – dark warnings about the dangers to humanity of trying to create a non-human super-intelligence, and that was my own first reaction. But I couldn't consider writing a story for six-to-nine year olds in which the computer killed everybody. I couldn't even have the people 'kill' the computer. The smart house was a potentially sympathetic character, even if it did pose a threat to the people who lived inside it, and I wanted a 'win-win' kind of ending. David, the little boy hero and narrator of the book, would succeed when the adults were helpless. He'd be the first to notice there was a problem; he'd try to escape, and fail; he'd figure out the problem, and then, finally, he'd provide the solution to make everybody happy.

I wrote and rewrote *Mad House*. It was hard fitting so much story into so few words. When I was satisfied, I sent it off. It came back with a detailed critique from the editor. Many of her comments were small things, easily dealt with, but one was major: she said the book needed many more small, humorous incidents. I knew she was right, but how on earth could I add any *more* when I'd already used up my allotted 8,000 words? The difficult job of trimming, pruning and reshaping began again. I could think up plenty more incidents, but each one had to be told concisely and efficiently (as well as amusingly), and the words to do it had to be whittled away from the scenes I'd already composed.

Having a responsive and thoughtful editor was vital – Cally Poplak, take a bow. In writing for adults, although I've frequently had sympathetic, helpful editors, I've never encountered the same level of hands-on involvement as in children's book publishing.

Young writers

After 'The Storms of Windhaven' – the novella which later became the first section of our novel *Windhaven* – was published in a science fiction magazine, George R. R. Martin and I were contacted by an editor who said her teenaged son had read our story twice, and she thought we could expand it into an excellent YA novel. Although we'd started talking about writing other stories set on Windhaven, with an idea of eventually weaving them together into a novel, the idea that it might be of particular interest to teenagers had not occurred to us. In retrospect, it's obvious. Our protagonist was a teenager, and it was a coming-of-age story, about a young woman who rebels against a stuffy, repressive society and forces it to change. I suppose we'd missed the obvious simply because we weren't far out of the young adult category ourselves (I was just 21). We wrote a story that *we* found compelling without trying to aim it at a particular age-group.

There is an idea that young writers may have a special understanding of and appeal to the young adult audience, and traditionally many fantasy and SF writers have started young. Most famously, perhaps, Mary Shelley wrote *Frankenstein* at the age of 19. Catherine Webb, currently one of Atom's leading authors, wrote her first novel, *Mirror Dreams*, when she was only 14, and four more books followed while she was still at school. However, although youth may be touted as a selling point, chronological age is less important to success in this field than having a youthful outlook and an active imagination.

9

Helping Yourself

There are no shortcuts to improving as a writer; there's only long practice. Write regularly, and read as much as you can. Rewrite what you've written and, when you feel it is as good as it can possibly be, send it out for publication. If it comes back, send it out again.

Ah, but what if it *keeps* coming back, and you can't see any way of making it better? If you think it's good, why doesn't anyone offer to publish it?

It can be difficult sometimes to see where – or if – you've gone wrong. Editors rarely have the time or inclination to go into detail about *why* they're returning your manuscript; rejections are usually polite, vague refusals. Trying to interpret a phrase like 'not quite right for our list' won't get you anywhere.

No matter how hard you try to bring a dispassionate, critical gaze to your own work, you can never really see it as a stranger. Always in your mind there's the book you *meant* to write, making it difficult to see what you've actually achieved. I never feel that a piece of writing is completely finished until it's been read by someone else. Often this is my husband (who has worked as a professional editor for more than 30 years); sometimes it's another writer, my agent, or the commissioning editor. Whoever the first reader, that outside eye is absolutely crucial. Writing is an act of communication, after all, and until it reaches an audience, any story is incomplete.

Ideally, the first reader is both sympathetic and informed, responsive to your intentions and to your writing, able to criticise the work intelligently and without wounding. Your first reader may be your husband, wife or best friend. However, loved ones may be *too* sympathetic to be genuinely helpful. They may

140

respond like a mother to her three-year-old's drawing, loving it because it's *yours*. Maybe they lack critical judgement, or can't distinguish between you and your work. They may feel (possibly rightly) that anything other than unqualified praise will hurt your feelings and damage the relationship. Maybe you don't want to risk that yourself. Some writers do like to keep their personal life separate from their writing – from their families they want unconditional, loving support, not literary advice.

Getting feedback

So, where can you go for help? Most cities and towns of any size will have some sort of writers' group you can join. Creative-writing classes are also a good way to meet other writers, get feedback on your work and hone your skills. Addresses for writing conferences, courses and workshops can be found in the annual *Writer's Handbook* or *Writers' and Artists' Yearbook*, and there's also a regularly updated directory of writers' circles around the country. These don't have to specialise in fantasy or science fiction to be helpful. However, some people *do* have a bias against genre fiction, so if you find yourself in a group where fantasy is despised, or members excuse themselves from commenting on your work because they 'don't understand' science fiction – get out. You don't need the aggravation, and constant negativity is worse than no feedback at all. And, luckily, there's another place to go to find people who under-stand what you're trying to do.

At the core of the SF and fantasy readership is the loosely organised group known as 'fandom'. If you're already a fan, you can skip the next two paragraphs. If not, consider getting involved. Fans have meetings and gather at annual conventions. Among the more regular conventions are the World Science Fiction Convention, the World Fantasy Convention, the British Fantasy Convention, Novacon, Eastercon, and lots more regional events. These 'cons' combine elements of fancy-dress party, informal social gathering, academic conference, and pub-crawl. Professional writers and editors are invited to give talks or readings and to sit on panel discussions. Some panels are serious; others much less so. Also on offer are video screenings, gaming, art shows, auctions, and book-stalls. Many convention-goers ignore the formal programme to spend all day socialising in the bar. This is a great place to meet other readers and aspiring writers, as well as professional writers, editors, agents, booksellers and artists.

A good first step towards finding out more about fandom, local fan groups and conventions is to join either the British Science Fiction Association (BSFA) or the British Fantasy Society (BFS) – or both. They have their own websites and produce various publications as well as holding meetings and informal gatherings, usually in London. These organisations offer a great way of keeping in touch with the SF and fantasy world, with regular listings of conventions, local fan groups, professional market reports, small press listings, book reviews, competitions, news and advice. (For contact details, see the end of the book.)

Through these organisations you should be able to get in touch with fans in your area and with the sub-group of fans who write. Even if there's no local writers' group, you should be able to link up with others online, where a lot of writing work-shops are conducted nowadays.

Courses and classes

Degree courses in creative writing have become increasingly popular in recent years. The appeal, to anyone longing for authorisation to concentrate on their writing, and, at the end of a set period, to be validated in some way as a writer, is obvious. However, while a degree may help you get a job as a teacher of creative writing, it certainly doesn't guarantee publication.

There's nothing in this country like the Clarion Science Fiction Writers' Workshop, founded in the United States more than 35 years ago. Now based on a campus in Seattle, Washington, it runs for six weeks in the summer, with a different professional writer (and at least one editor) acting as instructor each week. Mornings are usually devoted to classwork – writing exercises or a general discussion of some aspect of writing; afternoons to 'work-shopping' the stories written by the students. (Manuscripts are photocopied and distributed to everyone the day before.) The rest of the time is for writing, reading manuscripts, and individual conferences between students and instructors.

Writers who've attended Clarion tend to be enthusiastic proselytisers for it. As writing workshops go, it has a high rate of success, judging by the number of professional writers who have emerged from it. Spending six weeks surrounded by other writers, constantly writing, talking and thinking about writing, can be a life-changing experience.

But it is expensive, of course; even more so if you have to travel there from abroad. For most people, taking six weeks off from work and family obligations, paying for room, board and tuition to improve their writing skills, is not a realistic option.

Signing up for a short-term residential course, closer at hand, is another consideration. Writing centres such as Arvon and Ty Newydd offer four- and five-day courses, and grants are available to help defray the expense. Although most of the courses tend to concentrate either on poetry or on general fiction, there's usually at least one week dedicated to fantasy or science fiction. Other arts organisations may offer one-day or weekend workshops which can be very helpful as a way of making contact with other writers and getting feedback.

Starting a writers' circle

If you can't find one already in existence that suits, why not start your own? You may be able to meet compatible writers at conventions or on a writing course. Students who meet at Arvon (or elsewhere) often decide to keep in touch and read each other's work either through the post or via the Internet. If you are able to travel and can spend the occasional weekend away from home, you can get together for your own workshops.

I was one of the founder-members of Turkey City (full, improbable name: The Turkey City Science Fiction Writers' Workshop and Neo-Pro Rodeo) in Texas in the 1970s, and most of our members lived hundreds of miles apart. Bruce Sterling, Bill Wallace and I lived in Austin; Steven Utley was in one far-flung Dallas suburb (Carrollton) while Howard Waldrop and Jake Saunders lived in another (Prairie City); Joe Pumilia was down in Houston, while Tom Reamy's homestead was a ranch way out in West Texas. Perhaps three times a year we'd gather at someone's house with our manuscripts and spend the day arguing about what was wrong with them. We'd then party all night, so the problem of where everyone was to sleep didn't arise.

A decade later I became part of the newly formed Writers' Bloc in England – a different location, a different cast of characters (Christopher Evans, Garry Kilworth, R. M. Lamming, David Garnett, David Wingrove) but a similar MO – except for the all-night partying. We were older, and all within commuting distance of London, so we managed to get ourselves home again after spending all of Saturday workshopping.

The general routine for this sort of workshop follows below.

Preparation

Manuscripts, which can be either complete short stories or part of a work-in-progress, are copied and distributed to everyone a week in advance. A word-limit should be set – under 10,000 is sensible. It's a good idea to read each story at least twice and to take notes. My preference is to read it first fairly quickly and jot down my initial response: did I like it; did it make me laugh; were there any points where I was confused or bored. A day or so later I read it again, this time much more carefully. As I read I mark the manuscript, noting where I think the language is weak, unclear, repetitious, or particularly apt. I also look at the way the story fits together, listen to the dialogue, consider the believability of the characters and the construction of the plot. Is the ending satisfying? Does it all make sense? What sort of emotional charge does it carry, and does that reflect what the author seems to be trying to do? If I don't like something, I try to figure out *why*. Sometimes it may be personal prejudice – I don't like this character because he reminds me of my ex-husband! – so I try to be as objective as I can, and take the story on its own terms. I also make notes about things I especially liked, because nobody wants to hear only the bad news. And if I can't find anything wrong with the story, I try to figure out what makes it so good – being able to describe why one story works can be as helpful to a writer in the long term as suggesting details about what needs to be fixed in another.

Refrain from talking about the stories with anyone else – *especially* their authors – before the workshop.

On the day

Meet promptly at the time agreed. If long distances are involved, some members may have arrived the night before. Late-night partying beforehand is not advised, and *don't* talk about the stories! One person, probably the host, should take the role of facilitator and time-keeper and decide on the order of discussion. Each person will take it in turn to talk about the first story – but don't start with the same person every time; move around the circle. A time-limit should be agreed and kept to. Five minutes is generous; most people waffle or repeat themselves if given much more than that. Cutting it shorter can have a positive effect, as you will be forced to focus more clearly on what's important if you have only two minutes to get your ideas across. The author of the story under discussion is not allowed to interrupt or speak at all until everyone else has had their say. Then he or she is allowed five minutes to respond – also without interruption. After that, either a second round, or a less formal discussion among those who have the most to say, before moving on to the next story.

Numbers

This sort of workshop can accommodate groups of up to 20 people; however, for a one-day workshop the ideal size is between five and ten. It is difficult to do justice to more than six stories in one day. Ideally, every critic will also have contributed a story to be criticised, but in larger groups that's not possible.

Critical tips

If you have nothing to say about a story after you've read it twice and given it careful thought, don't agonise in public – just pass to the next person. If you can't say anything useful about *any* of them, you should drop out, but everyone is bound to meet the occasional story which simply leaves them cold. My first experience with that, shortly after arriving in England from America, was a humorous story about cricket-playing aliens … pass.

Don't waste time repeating what's already been said. It is frustrating to hear other people make every single brilliant observation you meant to make, but there's no point pretending they haven't already said it. That doesn't mean you shouldn't speak, but keep it short and simple: 'I agree with most of what's been said already – especially about the disappointing ending. I agree with Jasmine that you should change the title. I disagree with Sam about the sex scene – I thought it was very erotic, although maybe it *does* go on a bit too long.'

Be specific. It's depressing to be told that your beloved story is 'boring' – helpful to have the reason pointed out: 'The story would move faster if you cut out the suitcase-packing scene, and maybe you don't really need *four* trips into cyberspace, just two.'

Don't take up the group's time enumerating spelling, punctuation or grammatical mistakes, but mark those on your copy of the manuscript and give the marked copy to the author.

On the receiving end

Try not to take comments about your story as personal criticism, and don't make major life-decisions (like burning your novel or quitting your job) on the day after a workshop.

The story you take to a workshop should be one you expect to rewrite, but it should not be a rough first draft. Make it as good and polished as you can, as if you were submitting it to a magazine.

Remember that you have blind spots, and so does everyone else. Personal taste is just that. Nothing ever written has completely universal appeal, not even the Bible or *Harry Potter*.

Some people just won't like what you write, and you can't argue them into changing their minds. But even people who don't like your work can make useful suggestions, so don't dismiss everything they say out of hand.

Listen to what is said about other people's work and compare those comments with your own perceptions. This should help you judge their remarks about your work. Even intelligent readers can be wrong. You need to learn to recognise when a bit of criticism is apt, even if painful, and when you should ignore it.

Make your own notes and file them away with the manuscript. Let the experience settle before you actually sit down to rewrite your workshopped story. Then, when you look at your notes, certain comments will make more sense. But although you should listen to advice and suggestions, remember, this is *your* work, and you're not writing to order.

Agents

Do you really need an agent?

There's no doubt that editors give priority to manuscripts sent in by an agent – effectively, they've been given the stamp of approval by another professional. But, in a Catch-22 situation, unless you're already a published author, many agents won't even agree to consider your work. One science fiction writer I know told me that her agent received more than 1,200 queries a week. Clearly, making contact with an agent willing to consider taking on new clients is going to take a long time – time which might be better spent by sending your manuscript out to editors yourself.

It's not a good idea to approach editors with your book while you're looking for an agent. If, by the time an agent agrees to represent you, the manuscript has been rejected by half a dozen publishing houses, the agent may, justifiably, feel that there's no point in going on.

Unless you have an introduction from another client, or live in London and move in the sort of circles where you're likely to meet an agent at a dinner party, you'll just have to approach a likely-sounding agent in the same way as you would an editor. Literary agents are listed in *Writers' and Artists' Yearbook* and *The Writers' Handbook* along with their percentages (15–20% is usual), specialities and 'no-nos'. Read these carefully. A few agents may have a particular interest in fantasy, while others consider it beyond the pale. When you've chosen one, write a polite letter of enquiry, including a self-addressed and stamped return envelope for their reply. Don't send your manuscript until asked.

In *On Writing*, Stephen King gives an example of the sort of letter likely to get a good response from agents. His imaginary young writer lists his previous publications (short stories in little magazines) and awards, and in a brief paragraph describes the novel he's working on. He offers to send the first 80 pages if the agent is interested. According to King the letter succeeded because it was 'literate and well-spoken' and the author had put as much care into composing it as he would in writing a short story, and because he was able to provide a list of publications. One of the best selling-points you can have in attracting an agent (apart from your brilliant talents as a writer, of course!) is if you can list previous sales and awards.

You don't need an agent to market your short stories: in fact, most agents leave it to authors to deal with low-paying short-story markets themselves, although they will advise you about the contracts. If you haven't yet written a novel, don't bother looking for an agent. If your short stories are not only published but attract attention by winning awards and getting reprinted in 'Best of the Year' collections, you may find that an agent will approach *you*.

If you sell your first novel yourself, you'll be in a position of strength as regards getting an agent. Take your time to consider the options. Having a good agent can make all the difference to a writer's career, but it may be better to represent yourself rather than risk becoming entangled with the wrong agent when you're just starting out. Kristine Kathryn Rusch, a successful author in several genres, declares, 'Agents will not save you. Agents will not help you unless you already know how to help yourself …

The agent you can get as an unpublished writer is the agent you'll have to fire when you're published. (Generally.)'

Publishers

Be polite and professional in your approach, and don't expect over-worked editors to get back to you immediately – or even within three months. After six months you might reasonably write to ask (politely) about it.

Choose your publisher with care: keep up-to-date with what authors they currently publish and the readership they're aiming at. It's a waste of everyone's time to send a fantasy epic to an editor who specialises in literary fiction, or to an imprint which ceased publication two years ago.

Agent Antony Harwood offers three rules for submitting your work:

- *Rule 1*: Keep your covering note short. If you have nothing more to say than 'Here's my novel, please read it,' that's all you should say.
- *Rule 2*: Don't explain your novel. If it needs explaining, there's something very wrong with it.
- *Rule 3*: Use writing handbooks, and find out who'll be reading your manuscript. Most agents and publishers have websites, so it's easy to see whom they represent or publish. If there are particular reasons for your submitting to that particular agent or publisher, say so. Otherwise, *Rule 1* applies.

Format

Manuscript form has not changed much over the years, despite the move towards computerised writing, editing and publishing. No editor will consider a hand-written script, and if it is hard to read – a faded photocopy or typescript with a large number of hand-written changes – you should type or print out a fresh

149

copy to send out. Have mercy on the reader's eyes and don't use a weird font or one smaller than 12-point. It should be double-spaced, properly paragraphed, and on one side of the paper only. The pages should not be stapled or bound together; for short stories you can use a paper clip. Make sure all pages are numbered and have some identifying tag – your last name or a word from the title – at either the top or bottom of the page, just in case a cat knocks over the manuscript pile.

Sufficient return postage should be included, along with a suitably sized padded envelope, addressed to yourself. The alternative is to enclose a self-addressed, stamped envelope ('sase') for the editor's reply, and state that the manuscript itself is disposable. Disposable manuscripts are much more common and acceptable these days, although I think they should be used only for submissions sent abroad: if you can afford to print out a complete new copy of your manuscript for each submission, you can afford the postage to get it back. Editors have too much paper to recycle already. If you're sending something to America, it's now possible to obtain US postage online, from www.usps.com, and this might be preferable to using International Postal Orders which some American post offices don't seem to recognise.

Once a manuscript has been accepted for publication, you may be asked to provide the text on a disk in a specific format. However, sending a disk with your book or story is only asking for it to be lost, and don't even *think* of submitting by e-mail! Electronic markets may prefer electronic submissions, but never assume that this is the case. *Always* check submission guidelines, or ask, before sending anything out.

Covering letters

Manuscripts should always be accompanied by a brief letter. The shorter the better, really, especially for short stories. Much thought and agony has gone into the composition of covering letters by authors – including me, until I realised how much time I was wasting on a mere formality. Now I keep my covering letters short and businesslike, whether the editor is a personal friend or a complete stranger. Only the salutation differs: 'Dear Ellen' to my friend; 'Dear Ms Datlow' or 'Dear Ellen Datlow' if we're unacquainted.

Don't use the covering letter to describe the story or supply your life history. Especially do not make inflated claims for the brilliance of the story. You can't charm or bully an editor into liking it, and they may become annoyed enough to react against it if they think that's what you're trying to do. The time for listing your many accomplishments as a human being, and for relating fascinating anecdotes about how you came to write the story, is *after* you've sold it.

For books, the situation is a little different. If you're not represented by an agent, you may need to work a little harder at selling yourself. So, you should probably mention previous sales and any awards you may have won – or even come close to winning. ('My short stories have appeared in *Interzone* and *The Magazine of Fantasy and Science Fiction*. Last year, my novella 'Over the Moon' made the Hugo ballot and was short-listed for the World Fantasy Award.')

This is the sort of letter I write to accompany a short story:

Dear Ellen,

Enclosed is a new story, 'A Cold Dish', which I hope you'll consider for use on sci.fi.com. I look forward to hearing what you think of it.

With best wishes,

It may seem odd and unnecessary to write a letter which says nothing more than 'here is a story' – but I've heard editors complain about 'rude' authors who don't bother to include such a letter. I've also heard them groan about authors who go on and on, bragging about their accomplishments in other fields, and 'explaining' the story. As Dennis Etchison wrote in an announcement for his last anthology: 'I don't care who you are, what you have or have not published previously or whether we have ever met or corresponded or have friends or interests in common. Each manuscript will be judged solely on its merits and must speak for itself.'

So, be polite, keep it brief, and let the story explain itself.

On collaboration

Writers who write books together are relatively rare in mainstream, literary fiction, but much more common in the field of fantasy and science fiction. A few writers establish themselves as a team, like the husband-and-wife collaborators Mark and Julia Smith (their joint pseudonyms include Jonathan Wylie and Julia Grey) or David and Leigh Eddings, but it is more common for writers with separate careers to work occasionally with another writer for a particular project – Bruce Sterling and William Gibson writing *The Difference Engine*, for example, or the collaborative novels written by Larry Niven and Jerry Pournelle and by Stephen King and Peter Straub. Harlan Ellison and Howard Waldrop have both published entire collections of short stories they wrote in collaboration with various friends.

What's the appeal of collaborating? In my experience, it grew out of the contacts and links I had with other writers; the excitement we all shared about writing. We were all in our 20s, and at roughly the same stage of our careers. Collaborating was a kind of over-spill from our social lives. We were both competitive with and supportive of each other. In our letters and whenever we got together, we talked about what we were writing, what we were reading, what we intended to write, and ideas were tossed back and forth. Stories were started on the spur of the moment, at a party or after a workshop. Someone would write a first page and hand it, like a challenge, to another writer. Most of what resulted was not very good, but we had fun writing it.

Occasionally two people will find that they work better together than they do separately. Their particular strengths and weaknesses may be well-matched; they keep each other inspired and encouraged. In some collaborations, one writer actually does all, or most, of the actual writing, with the other author contributing plot outlines and determining details about the background and characters.

Writing can be a lonely, solitary business. I suspect that most writers actually like it that way, or they'd do something else. Collaboration removes the solitude, but also the solitary pride. It doesn't suit everyone. The benefits of having someone to share the hard work with has to be balanced against the loss of complete control. (You have to split the money, too, of course.) Compromises must be made, and the end result is a work that neither one of you can wholly claim. If it's successful, it should be something neither partner could have written alone. It should really appear to be the work of a third, new author with a distinctive style.

Quotations

Sometimes writers like to use a few lines by another writer as chapter-headings, or even to include a brief quotation from another book within the body of the text. As long as this is properly acknowledged somewhere within the book it should not be a problem. You shouldn't need formal permission or have to pay a fee to quote a few lines from a novel, although it is a courtesy to inform the author and/or original publisher of your intention to quote.

However, this only applies to quotations which are too short to form 'a significant part' of the original copyright work. This means that although you can safely quote several lines or even whole paragraphs from a novel, even a single line is a 'significant part' of a poem. Unless the poem is out of copyright (which usually runs for up to 75 years after the author's death) you will need to get written permission from the publisher, and you may be required to pay a fee for its use.

If you are thinking of quoting from a popular song, my advice is to forget it. Publishers usually require the author to clear and pay for all necessary permissions: that means you'll have to track down the copyright-holder (who is not necessarily the performer or the songwriter) and negotiate terms – which may be ruinously high. Stephen King could afford to pay for all the songs he wanted to quote in *Christine*; George R. R. Martin found it more difficult when he had to clear permission for the songs he wanted to quote in *Armageddon Rag* – it took him months of hard work, cost a lot of money, and even then some had to be dropped when he couldn't reach agreement with a few copyright-holders. He swore he'd never include actual rock-song lyrics in anything he wrote in future.

So ask yourself: is this quotation really necessary?

10
Advice from Editors

It's all very well for one professional author to offer advice on how to write, based on her own experiences – and I certainly hope you've found something useful to you in the preceding pages. But what most unpublished writers really want to know is: What do editors want? How can I improve my chances of getting one of them to buy – or even read – my manuscript?

The market has changed a lot since I began writing professionally back in the 1970s. It's changed even since the first edition of this book, and will undoubtedly continue to change, but most of the advice given below should remain sound for years to come. For the record, the interviews were conducted by e-mail in August and September 2004. My survey group consisted of the heads of all the major SF & Fantasy lists in Britain, plus one small press:

Peter Crowther, PS Publishing
Jo Fletcher (position shared with Simon Spanton), Gollancz (Orion Publishing Group)
Tim Holman, Orbit and Atom (Time Warner Books UK)
Jane Johnson, Voyager (HarperCollins)
Peter Lavery, Tor (Macmillan)

First of all, do any of you still read unsolicited manuscripts, or does the writer have to have an agent before you'll take a look?

Jane Johnson: We can no longer take on unsolicited manuscripts; we just don't have the time or manpower for this. All publishing companies are now run on something of a skeleton staff; given the current strictures of the marketplace we're buying far less than we ever used to do, and the likelihood of finding a gem in the 'slush pile' is tiny. Agents are the only way forwards now for most committed writers: plus, we're more likely to take a submission from an agent seriously because there's already been a degree of selection and an investment in time and effort by another professional.

Tim Holman: We do consider unsolicited manuscripts – and all unsolicited submissions are looked at – but a good agent will help to make a submission stand out. Although having a good agent helps, finding one can be as difficult as finding a publisher.

Jo Fletcher: Yes, I do look at unsolicited manuscripts: Roger Taylor, Alastair Reynolds, Marian Veevers, and my new guys, Robert Scott and Jay Gordon, were all 'slush pile'. Two I read because we had friends in common, but none of them were agented. On the other hand, that's only four authors (Scott and Gordon are a team) in nearly 20 years! So yes, it can happen, and it does, but it is very *very* rare.

Peter Lavery: Yes, I definitely look at unsolicited material, if only briefly. In this genre it tends to be better focused and better written than the majority of the 'slush pile' submissions. We have taken on several such manuscrips over the last five years. I don't think it's vital, therefore, for an aspiring author to have an agent – but if they do, it should be someone who understands what they are writing and can therefore advise on and constructively help their careers.

Peter Crowther: As far as books are concerned I think it's absolutely essential for authors to have an agent. At PS (or should I say *even* at PS) we receive between half a dozen and ten requests each week to consider a new novel or collection or novella (PS's specialty), and, alas, I generally turn them down because I just don't have the time to read them all; nor do I want to take up my assistant editor's time reading what is, in effect, a slush pile. To this end, an agent is invaluable. No agent worth his or her salt is going to trawl around Publishers' Row with a clunky, badly written, badly plotted and badly presented work – thus, a manuscript coming in from an agent comfortably negotiates the first hurdle.

Having said all the above, I have broken my own rule (hell, it's my rule so I'll break it when I want) and bought books from people who approached me with an idea and, in a moment of weakness, I've asked them to send me a couple of chapters. Tracy Knight's *The Astonished Eye*, Robert Freeman Wexler's *In Springdale Town*, and, just this past week, Mark Samuels' *The Face of Twilight* to name but three – and every one of them absolutely stunning in my opinion. But it is important to emphasise that this is very rare, and I still reject more than half of them.

As regards short stories, I think an agent gets in the way. The vast bulk of stories I've accepted (for my 20-odd anthologies and for *Postscripts* magazine) have come direct from the author concerned. From my own point of view as a writer, I have a US and a UK agent. I use them for longer works and film options. I handle the short stories myself.

Can you describe the sort of novels you are looking for or like best?

Jo Fletcher: No! I'll know it when I see it! We're not looking for horror right now, because that market is still in a state of torpor; I hope it will recover. I like good writing, fantastic plot, excitement, emotion – all the things one looks for in any decent piece of writing.

Jane Johnson: I love really good fantasy novels with powerful characters, big plots and an engaging voice: the three I'd hold up as authors I'm particularly proud to publish in this area are Robin Hobb, George R. R. Martin and David Zindell. It's hard to pinpoint exactly what we're looking for, since we're not seeking to fill slots: the Voyager list is pretty much self-propelling at this point; so really it's a matter of originality, verve, and that indefinable thing which makes a reader keep turning the pages. In the end, great story-telling is the most crucial thing, whether it be a story set in a quasi-medieval world, in space, or in the future.

Peter Lavery: Mostly I look out for new and interesting ideas combined with a high level of writing.

Tim Holman: Orbit publishes a very wide range of genre fiction, and there is an equally wide range of qualities we're looking for in new fiction – but there always has to be a great story.

Peter Crowther: I'm a softie, so I'm a sucker for poignancy ... and I like to be amazed. Thus, I love material by the old greats – particularly Ray Bradbury. In SF, I want to be awed. In fantasy I want either to be transported to some otherworldly and perhaps even mythical (but believable) region, or I want to have the usual touchstones of contemporary society blurred in a surreal way (please note: I prefer no elves or dragons in either case), and in horror I want to be scared. Would-be writers should distinguish between 'scared' and 'made nauseous.' Make me smile, make my eyes go wide, make me wonder what that creak was, make me say, Wow!

Are there any particular types of books you'd rather never see again?

Tim Holman: No, as anything I say here is guaranteed to become the Next Big Thing!

Jane Johnson: The really derivative elves-and-dragons sagas, of which we see plenty; but equally, grim dystopic SF set in the UK 30 years hence; or Gibson-esque cyberspace caper-movie rip-offs – very *passé* now.

Peter Lavery: Excessively derivative, plodding, unfocused ones.

Jo Fletcher: Series 'tie-ins'. Cat fantasies (that's Simon's, but I'm with him!) – in fact, anthropomorphic fantasies of any type. 'Erotic' SF.

Peter Crowther: I was bored with splatter-punk/gore, etc. almost as soon as it was becoming recognised for what it was – in other words, Excess. And I quickly get bored of swear-words when used – or mis-used – by people who should know better. If we use food as an analogy for writing, then profanity is like a garnish: use it only on the meal that requires it and use it sparingly, lest you lose the taste of the actual food itself.

What are some of the most common mistakes made by aspiring but unsuccessful SF or fantasy writers?

Tim Holman: The same mistakes made by other writers, I suspect. Regarding the writing itself, the most common one, I think, is to over-write: to imagine that their prose style is going to be admired for its own sake; and to include material – sentences, paragraphs, chapters – that might be brilliant but gets in the way of the story and does not contribute to the novel as a whole.

Regarding submissions, covering letters and synopses should be short and to the point. Very few editors would read a three-page letter introducing a novel, and it's not necessary to include suggestions for marketing, cover art, movie potential, etc.

Peter Crowther: Being derivative and not original. I know, I know … it sounds like a *Blue Peter* solution: 'How to be a great writer – jolly well write greatly!' But it's absolutely true. We all wear our influences on our sleeves – particularly when we're new to the game – but it's absolutely essential to get to work on developing your own 'voice' as soon as possible.

Jo Fletcher: In genre, particularly, thinking that using weird, unpronounceable names makes it SF or fantasy.

Working so hard to make their world fully rounded that they forget about plot or characterisation.

'Borrowing' someone else's world ('I just loved Buffy and got to thinking, hey, wouldn't it be neat if she started dating Homer Simpson ...').

Not knowing what's gone before: you might have what you think is the most original idea in the world, but chances are it's been done before. The publishers do know the history of the genre and will spot it a mile off.

Thinking a book has to be 300,000 words long or a trilogy to sell.

And generally (this goes for all writers) thinking they *deserve* to be published because their Great Aunt Mabel, their kid brother or their cat 'loved' their book. Asking for advice from editors – and then throwing a tantrum when they get it. *Not* checking out writers' manuals and guidelines – they're there for a reason. Thinking that a good story will win over bad spelling and poor presentation. Hand-writing anything. Binding a submission manuscript. Forgetting to double-space and paragraph properly. Expecting an answer within a week, or a month. Thinking they can write better than Jeffrey Archer – and that therefore their work must be publishable!

Peter Lavery: Sending bits and pieces of a novel as 'samples' of style or narrative; using tiny type without proper spacing. Editors haven't got the time or inclination to interpret confusion or go blind in the process. Beyond that, hassling by phone or e-mail within days of submission. That's likely to produce a swift rejection just to get some peace.

Jane Johnson: The same mistakes made by writers in any area – being too derivative; trying to write for a perceived marketplace; telling rather than showing; too much detail; not enough dialogue; superficial, unsympathetic characters; burying the story in fancy tricks; lack of clarity.

What advice would you give a new writer?

Peter Lavery: Perfect your skill and style as best you can before submitting, and then be persistent. Because when a publisher says 'no', it may be more to do with an overloaded list than with the quality of the submission itself.

Jane Johnson: Write whenever you can, about all sorts of things. As with every other skill, practice is crucial. Read widely. Travel, even if only to the other side of your own town. Carry a notebook. Listen to people, take an interest in them (although there's a line to be drawn between listening and eavesdropping!); practice writing dialogue – it can move a narrative along at a swift pace and delineates characters – you should be able to hear your characters and picture them in your head.

Peter Crowther: Read. Write – short stories, not novels. Every day. And always have something out there somewhere, being considered.

Tim Holman: Only do it if you find the writing itself a rewarding experience. Assume that your novel will not be published.

Jo Fletcher: Write for yourself. If you get published, that's a bonus. Write to the absolute best of your ability at all times, but remember: this should be a pleasure. Write every day. Read. Look at how published writers structure books, deal with plot and character.

On submission: check out the writers' manuals. Know your field. *Finish the book* before submitting it. Check out the name of the current editor (I'm still getting manuscripts addressed to publishers who died nearly a decade ago, and to colleagues who have long, long since moved on. It takes one phone call; how hard is that?). Don't submit by e-mail unless invited to do so. Always include return postage or state that the manuscript is a disposable copy.

Most importantly: *Don't give up the day job!* No matter how good you are (or think you are), until you're several books in and have been selling an increasing number of copies each time, trying to live solely on your writer earnings is tantamount to suicide. (And if you're a poet, like me, don't even think it in your dreams!)

Would you care to hazard any predictions about the future of fantasy & SF as a genre?

Tim Holman: I suspect there will be more active integration of SF and fantasy into mainstream fiction by publishers and booksellers – as we've seen with crime and horror.

Peter Lavery: I'm sure there will be room in future for both good 'traditional category' writing and the more 'experimental' and innovative, but I imagine that the more distinctive a voice in either area, the sooner it will be heard.

Jane Johnson: Hard to distinguish between the genre of and as itself and as a player in the modern book marketplace: all I can say about the latter is that times are tough, the book chains are not as supportive of new writers in this area as they should be, and the market is flat.

Jo Fletcher: Myths and legends have been part of humankind's heritage since the first story-teller shambled over to the fire, and I can see no reason why that should change. There are advantages to lumping together all these different types of imaginative fiction and calling it F&SF, one of which is that the fans know what to look for, but there are also disadvantages: on the whole it is easier to get huge sales for a mainstream book rather than for one labelled SF, but it's also easier to get steady sales and repeating backlist sales for genre publications. We've been debating the value of independent lists for decades, and I imagine we will continue to do so.

On the whole, Simon and I think there are more advantages

to being published as a genre author than not. It's possible to be a mid-list fantasy or SF author and survive, because this is pretty much the only place a mid-list still exists, due to the backlist. It means they can survive without the massive hype (and consequent massive marketing costs) that mainstream authors need for their often all-too-brief place in the sun.

We survive because we have a dedicated fan-base and we do well not to forget that.

Peter Crowther: I think it's very rosy indeed, but then I'm a 'glass half full' type of fellow and not a 'glass half empty' one. The whole publishing world is going through a period of readjustment and we just have to move along with it. I'm fascinated by the increasingly important role played by the specialty presses in our field. It's very encouraging: I'm not just talking about PS, but look at the wonderful quality of books put out by Cemetery Dance, Subterranean, Golden Gryphon and NightShade ...

Of the three areas in fantastical fiction (SF, fantasy and horror) I believe that horror will continue to struggle. It'll improve, because it has to change; the old staples (vampires, monsters, etc.) will give way to new takes and new writers. I'm not going to be so reckless as to name names, but I think we're already seeing work from many of them.

Fantasy will continue to get a boost from *The Lord of the Rings* and other movies, but I hope we're not heading for more umpteen-volume sagas: time will tell.

SF will continue to flourish simply because it's the literature of ideas. You can consider anything in SF: population changes, environment changes, Godhood, life after death, alien encounters, time travel, life on other planets ... you name it.

11
The Story of a Story

My first novel, *Windhaven*, was written in collaboration with George R. R. Martin. It began as a short story, published as 'The Storms of Windhaven'. Although I'd collaborated with other writers before, this was the longest and most ambitious project yet. I had always been a fairly instinctual writer, allowing my stories to develop as I wrote them rather than beginning with any firm plan. Working with another person, someone who wrote and thought differently from myself, was an eye-opening experience. It taught me a lot about how stories work. For the first time, I had to explain, and sometimes justify, my feelings about plot, character, language, names ...

Usually, deconstructing a story relies on a lot of guesswork. Even when a first draft exists, full of hand-written changes and crossings-out, the original imaginative work is invisible, inaccessible, thoughts inside a head. In a collaboration, much of that normally invisible process is verbalised. In the case of 'The Storms of Windhaven', written by two authors living in different places (George was in Chicago; I was first in Houston, then in Los Angeles), a lot of it was written down in an exchange of letters.

I thought it might be interesting to reprint part of our discussion here, as an illustrated example of how one story got written. Generalisations about writing can take the novice writer only so far: what is most helpful is specific advice aimed at a particular piece of work. Since that's not something a book can provide, maybe an example will be helpful. You can compare and contrast what George and I said to each other with various pronouncements I've made throughout this book. If you'd like to read 'The Storms of Windhaven', it appears as the section titled 'Storms', Part One of *Windhaven*.

The proposal came from George, something from his files he referred to as an 'idea germ' – no characters, no plot, no scenes, just the beginning of something he thought might be worked up into an SF story. This was it:

An ocean planet; the only land is small, scattered, rocky islands, a few big enough to farm on. A ship crashes. It's a Cordwainer Smith-Arthur Clarke kind of sail ship, with immense metal wings, never meant to land. There are survivors, but they become primitive in a few generations, as there is no metal for a technology. However, the immensely strong, immensely light cloth-metal of the sailship sail has survived. Since the ocean is wracked by storms, volcanic activity, and is very dangerous to sail (dinosaurs?!), the early survivors, who still had some tools, cut up the metal cloth into glider-type one-man wings. They fly on strong storm-wind currents, from island to island. The wings are handed down. Family heirlooms. The flyers, naturally, are glamorous figures. It's dangerous, they're the only ones who travel, etc.; much more exciting than the drudgery of growing food, etc. Conflict. Maybe twins in one family. A primogeniture tradition, but now, who gets the wings? 'On the Wings of Storm' sounds like a nice title.

I responded:

Oh, I've got it. How's this. For the 'On the Wings of Storm' story (and incidentally I don't like that title, it sounds like a comic book or a soap opera or [heaven forbid] a gothic, so let's try to get another, okay?). The tradition would likely be (you mentioned primogeniture) the wings going to the eldest son (unless he were absolutely unfit to fly). So, a family in which the male children have been still-born, died in infancy, or not born at all, so there is only the one girl-child and her parents are getting old – not likely to have a son, so they must train her to carry on. She's maybe 11. She gets to fly, fantastic. Her mother gives birth again, a son who lives, and she dies giving birth. So the girl has to kind of take over being a mother, but goes on learning to fly because they don't expect the boy to live. But he does, and grows up healthy, and the day is going to have to come when he learns to fly. In fact, as the father is probably a doddering old wreck by this time (the tough life on this planet ages them all quickly) the girl does much of the teaching, just as she does more flying now than the father and has begun to look upon the wings as hers. But they are the father's – he is going to give them to his son when the boy is old enough and skilled enough and the girl has to watch her whole life coming to an end – she simply doesn't *want* to give up the air to raise babies and cabbages with a farmer husband. She may reach a point where she thinks of killing the boy, but he is almost as much her son as brother and she loves him, while hating what he is forcing her to become. I don't know how it will end, but it don't look too bright from this end, George.

I'm not sure about the women not flying ... in most matters in this society the men and the women are equal – they're all for the most part subsistence farmers ... they grow what they can, and they gather bird eggs, hunt birds, gather mussels, crabs, do some fishing, I don't know what all ... I doubt there are any animals on land, just air and sea creatures. In matters of inheritance, the women rank with younger sons. There is no reason why women can't fly, it's simply inheritance laws, and the mystique of flying keep flyers as an in-group, initiating only their heirs into the privilege. The girl has belonged to this world and so is going to have to give up her closest friends as well as her wings to her brother.

This is all pretty much off the top of my head ... How many flyers to an island? For that matter, how many people?

Let me know what you think ...

George's response to this was enthusiastic, and my ideas sparked more in him:

We should work out some cultural reason why the wings can't be shared – otherwise the reader will just mutter something like, 'Why don't they take turns?'

More planet culture. Look, instead of the flyers being the *only* communication between islands, let's say they have boats, too. Fishing boats at least, maybe ferries; all wind- or oar-powered, though, since there is no technology. The flyers are still the glamour-boys, though, as they're much faster. And the seas are full of dangerous animals. Also frequent violent storms, which a skilled flyer can use to his advantage, while the ships are wiped out. The flyers maybe have built a lodgehouse or something on a rocky island that can only be reached by air (high plateaus like Devil's Island so no ships could moor); a transfer-point for goods and messages, a resting place. We can use it as a symbol of the flyer-society our heroine will be denied, since she'll be totally cut off from it without wings.

Endings. I can think of a bunch. None of them completely satisfy me. One, she could give up the wings, try to reconcile herself to it. The moral would be 'sometimes you have to give up dreams'. Pfagh. I just wrote that in 'Fast-Friend', and I'm not sure I believe it. Too damned grown-up and realistic. Alternatively, she could fly away. Just take the wings and go, run to some other island where a flyer would be appreciated, where her origins aren't known, where she won't have to face her brother and father. That's better, but I still don't like it much. Three, a variant: she just flies off over the sea to die. Death is better than life without wings. Four, wings get damaged and broken so nobody can have them (cheat! cheat!). Five, it turns out the son didn't want to be a flyer. He has some other dream, and is just being pushed into flying by his father's expectations. Six, she kills the kid. Seven, she finds some way to build another pair. Eight, she kills a second flyer to get an extra pair. Nine, she becomes a nun and flies with the aid of a giant hat.

I think I like numbers 2, 3 and 5 the best. But I'm very receptive for improvements. Suggest away.

Titles. Hmmm. Maybe 'Stormwings'? Or 'My Brother's Wings'? Or 'God is My Flock-Mate'? Or 'The Winds Are Not For Me'? 'Stormfever'? 'Flying Fever'? Something like that. How about 'The Secret Storm' or 'Death-Duel in a Stormy Sky'? (*That'll* teach you to call my title soap-opera-ish or comic-bookish, even if it was ...)

I replied:

I'll start on 'Stormwings' (or whatever) maybe tomorrow ... I am really interested in it, as I am in nothing else that I have in mind to write. As for the ending, I think I like Number 5: the boy doesn't want to be a flyer at all, he wants to be (perhaps) a writer or storyteller or the equivalent (a singer? By the way, do they have books? Printed or only hand-written?) And is actually terrified of flying (which the girl has never considered – to her, it is inconceivable that anyone could fear this, the greatest thing in the world) but has been learning because it is expected of him and nobody ever asks the son of a flyer if that is what he wants to be, too. When he admits his feelings to the girl they work something out – perhaps they go away *together* to another island where she can be a flyer and he can do his thing and there will be no shame attached to either of them ... have to work this out ...

I'll start writing on it and see what I can get done, then send it to you for suggestions, additions, improvements and we'll carry on like that. Okay?

I like 'Wings' for a title, but unfortunately Vonda [McIntyre] already used it. Well, we'll see what develops. Search poetry for ideas.

Five days later I had written ten pages and sent them to George with this:

Your turn now. Take it from here, and of course feel free to make any changes you like in the existing part (and if I don't like them I will only rip out your guts with my teeth).

I'm feeling very good. I haven't felt so happy writing a story for some time – also, it all came very easily (up to the point where I stopped, which is as I was about to introduce Coll).

You will notice that I changed my mind about having the law of inheritance be to the eldest son. That's so Old Earth, and I kept thinking of Vonda grinding her teeth, so I decided better it should have nothing to do with sex-discrimination.

Feel free to change any names of persons places things. I especially have trouble with what to name local animals ... a sea monster is a sea monster, but what would the locals call it that would be obvious without requiring an explanation to the simple reader? 'You bellow like a sea-bull' says someone – which isn't exactly what I wanted, but alternatives like 'a pacu' or 'a glbzzk' sounded ludicrous. I don't really like the name Flan and I don't know why I used it. (It is a Spanish dessert, is what it is – the same thing that you had for dessert at that Greek place, only of course the Greeks don't call it flan.) If you have a better name you can insert it. Also, I realised after writing him in that the character Tor has no purpose and doesn't even say anything – I put him in as company for Gina, I guess, but we really don't need him.

Let me know what you think about this ... please write some more ... you can finish it if you like and then send it to me for additions and excisions. I think Coll is going to hand over the wings to Maris on his coming-of-age day, but I haven't worked out all the ramifications of that – you are welcome to (she said kindly) – I will certainly let you know if I object to anything.

A few notes to explain the above: I'd become friendly with the writer Vonda McIntyre at Clarion. I admired her very much, and shared her feminist convictions, although I was rarely as outspoken and straightforward about my beliefs as she was. (As here, for example; pretending I was concerned about Vonda's reaction to a fictional sexist set-up rather than simply admitting that I, myself, was fed up with stories that perpetuated old-fashioned patriarchal social systems. After all, if science fiction writers couldn't present a plausible, sexually egalitarian society, what hope was there for changing the real world?)

At this point we were both thinking of this as a short story – probably under 6000 words – rather than the novella that 'Storms of Windhaven' became; we certainly didn't conceive of it as the beginning of a novel. Hence, my concern about having included an 'unnecessary' character like Tor. 'Extras' clutter short stories to no purpose, but they add richness to longer works. 'Storms of Windhaven' is full of examples of bits of local colour and extra characters which, while they might at first have seemed disposable, became more important later on – even suggesting later story developments.

George's reply to my opening soon arrived:

Oh, wow. Yes. You should be happy. I love it. This is going to be one hell of a story ... I can see it now. I hope they make twin Hugos, so we won't have to pass one back and forth. Really.

In other words, I'm enthusiastic. I just got your mss today, and just finished reading it, and I can hardly wait to go on. It was invigorating just reading the thing; one of the nice things about collaborations. The writing seems tremendously fresh and strong and vivid, minus my typical stylistic quirks that would've dotted it if I'd done that part. Ah, but this is going to be good.

But enough raves. Idea time, so I'll talk about the story. Animal names I think I can handle; I'm pretty good at that. The best way to handle it, I think, is to avoid naming things gizzuks and smerps, and to run together real words and use them in context in such a way that they're self-explanatory. Besides, human colonists would *never* name anything a gizzuk. Thusly I have stories that feature wind-wolves and tree-spooks and rock-cats and plains-devils and such. One idea for your sea monster – how 'bout calling them scyllas? Or has that been done? Something like that anyway ...

I mostly love the section you sent me; only a couple of changes I'd like to make. For one thing, I'd like to expand the opening flight scene – have Maris in the air for, say, two pages, instead of two graphs – with more description of sea and sky and such. I don't think we'll lose the reader; the concept is exciting enough to be a narrative hook. The names are mostly okay, but I really hate Flan, which reminds me of Spam somehow, which is not a proper association. Of course, naming characters after Greek foods is a long-established tradition. Silverberg has written about men named Metaxas (*Up the Line*) and Roditis (*To Live Again*) both of whom are really Greek wines ... still. How about Lind? Dorrel? Or anything but Spam ...

How are you at poetry? A scene has come to mind ... A singing scene, of course. Two ballads are performed. One, an old traditional epic, tells of the fall of the sailship and the fashioning of the first wings, thus sneaking in a bunch of background while giving us a good feel for the legends and culture of the planet. Then after the Singer has finished, young Coll takes the guitar or whatever and does a song of his own composition ... an ode to the joy of flying. Maris completely misinterprets the song, reading in it an echo of her own lust for the sky, missing the obvious love with which Coll sings. Yes, yes, yes ... but how shall we write it? From a distance, only describing the songs? Or close up, giving the texts? I'm terrible at poetry, but if you're good, maybe you could take a crack at it and write two songs.

Just make sure the ode to flying doesn't begin with 'Off she goes, into the wild blue yonder ...'

I'm also going to try to do some more detail work on the wings, in terms of description of their construction,

wingspan, etc. If I can figure it all out. We can give the
planet low gravity, but the wings would still have to be
pretty damn big. How big are hang-gliders, anyhow? I'll
have to look that up – I think I saw a photo in *Time*.

In any case, I will do something on it, a lot I hope, and
bring it with me to LA. If there's an extra typewriter there
we should be able to whip through the final draft while
we're together, I hope.

I replied:

I'm DELIGHTED you love the story as much as I do and
will look forward to seeing whatever you may have done
or will want to do when you reach LA. Change Flan's
name to Dorrel, okay?

I can't write poetry ... I could try, I suppose, to write a
song, but dunno if it would be any good.

I agree with you about extending the opening scene
with Maris in the sky – I thought of that myself, but I
rarely do extended descriptive writing so I decided to leave
that up to you. (I figured you'd mention it.)

Together in LA, we wrote and discussed more of the story, but
didn't manage to finish writing it – although we were agreed on
how it should end, and had started to think we might want to
write more stories set on the same world. They might even make
a 'fix-up' novel. After George left, I wrote him a letter which
included some details about glider-flying (I'd done some
research), outlined an idea for 'the second story in our series'
which was to feature a wingless former flyer who builds himself
a wooden glider (this story, which would have changed our
fictional world rather dramatically, was never written) and
enquired:

By the way, what's the name of our planet? If you get any
more information on it (from spirit voices from Jupiter, or
wherever) be sure to let me know and I'll do the same for

you. As for a title, how about 'To Give Up The Sky' or
'The Taste of Flight'? So, okay, now it's your turn to make
suggestions.

When I'm done with it, I'll send the story to Chicago.

Somewhere along the way – whether it was George or me or the
spirit voices from Jupiter, no letter records – our planet got
named Windhaven. When I'd finished and George had made
any additional changes he wanted, he took the story (still without a firmly agreed title) to a Turkey City down in Texas.
According to his report, everybody there loved it, so I showed it
to Ben Bova, editor of *Analog*, when I met him during his visit
to LA. Since he'd already bought stories from George (but not
from me), I had high hopes he'd take it immediately.

He didn't.

Although he thought it had a great beginning, and he loved
the world we'd created and the story situation, Ben said it was
too talky, and the ending was far too weak to be satisfactory. As
he quite reasonably pointed out, Maris won too easily. There
was no real conflict in our story, only a brief misunderstanding.
Maris wants the wings and Coll wants to give them to her, and,
as it turns out, nobody really minds. But no tradition worthy of
the name would collapse so easily. And if there *was* no powerful
tradition, no real opposition to Maris keeping the wings, then
what was the story? If we rethought the plot – basically went
back and made life a lot more difficult for our heroine – he said,
he'd like to see it again.

I don't have any letters recording our first reaction to this;
probably George and I talked about it over the phone. I know
we saw the justice in Ben's objections, but still felt we had a
good story and, having moved on to other ideas, rather resented
having to rework it. We decided we'd beef up the opposition to
Maris as non-flyer-born being allowed to keep the wings, show
that she really had a fight on her hands, and then give her a
powerful argument to let her win.

I wrote a new final scene and sent it to George. He replied at
length:

I've read over your rewritten talk scene, and thought about it.

Lisa, it's not going to work.

Oh, the scene is fine enough, very well written, but I don't think the story would hold up very well structurally if we went that way. As it is, we've got structural problems. Garth and Dorrel, who are dominant characters early in the story, really don't *do* anything of permanent importance, if you stop to analyse the plot. Barrion, who will become a really major character if we try to introduce this jealousy angle, isn't introduced until page 20. Of a 30-page story. The dramatic confrontation – the conflict – will be Maris and Coll and Barrion trying to change Russ's mind, and any such scene is bound to be a lot of talk, no matter how we write it. That's one of the problems with the story as it now stands.

The Woodwings song is a very nice thing, but I'm worried about that. We really can't have Coll writing *too* many songs, unless we want to turn it into a hootenany. If we use the Woodwings song, we'd have to cut the song about Raven. And without *that* and its effect, then Raven and that whole flashback has no dramatic purpose. We'd have to cut that.

Also, I don't know if the party scene has any dramatic purpose at all, with the way we're doing this story now. We'd have to cut that, with all the songs, etc.

You realise, of course, that everything above is rationalisation. My real reasons for objecting so loud is that I wrote in Raven and I wrote in those songs and I love them and dammit I don't want to take them out. They're pretty. I'm proud of them. They're part of the reason everybody at Turkey City loved the story, I think. But I don't want to leave them in if there is no function to be served – that makes them just debris from an earlier story that was going in a different direction, and some sharp-eyed readers are bound to notice this.

So. Now that I've gotten you all depressed, I'm going to

cheer you up (I hope) with some new, exciting proposals
that will hopefully make the story better than ever, and get
us both enthusiastic about it. Look, we both hate
rewriting, right? Especially on this story, which we think
we've finished, right? And we (plus the Turkey City
people) like what we have now, although we agree about
what Ben says, too, right? So: I propose we keep nearly
everything we have now, but save the story by lengthening
it. Considerably. A novella, Lisa. Maybe 18–20,000
words. It alone can be a good chunk of the novel version,
and it stands a good chance to win Nebulae or Hugos,
since this will be damn good and there *aren't* that many
novellas published. Even bad ones.

And ours will be dynamite.

So. First of all, look at pages 14–15. Particularly at
Dorrel's speech that begins on the bottom of 14, and Maris'
answer to it. That's the focus of the new idea. We assume
that Maris knows – *has* known, for a long time – that Coll
wants to sing. But both of them are trapped by tradition, by
law. A stupid tradition, since bad flyers die each year, and
the number of wings grows less. Eventually the system will
destroy communication unless it is changed.

We let the first 20 pages stand exactly as is (I've made
your corrections already) ... and start rewriting, briefly,
where you did: the sand-candle talk between Coll and
Maris. But not the rewrite that you have now. Instead, a
conversation that fully reveals to the reader that both of
them want Maris to fly, Coll to sing. But both don't know
how to do it, both are bowed by the weight of tradition,
of which their father is a symbol. Don't mention
Woodwings here; we can keep the original.

On page 21, we resume after the scene change ('The
week went on forever ...') and keep all that, intact, all the
way through the party. We keep the singing pretty much
as is – delete only Maris' thoughts about how this proves
that Coll wants to fly, instead substituting thoughts like,
'He sings the way I fly – with love,' etc. Finally, when he

175

does Raven's Fall, Maris is resolved. He has given a song to the world, a beautiful new song – it is not fair that he should be denied the life he wants, she the one she wants, etc., because of stupid tradition.

So, we've kept nearly the entire story.

But start the expansion from the point where I had Maris run away. Everything after that gets junked. Instead we substitute a rewritten scene much like the one you did out in LA, the one Ben read: a wing presentation rite, etc. But Coll does not refuse the wings or give them to Maris – he's only a 13-year-old kid, trying to do what's expected. He takes them dutifully, if without joy. The party adjourns to flyer's cliff for his first flight. It is a very clumsy flight. In landing, he tilts, a wing hits the ground, a strut shatters (damage, yes, but easily repaired – it's only a small tragedy, more embarassing than anything else). But Coll rises white-faced, terrified, crying ... Coll blurts out something that shocks the party (I don't *want* your wings), Russ gets stern, and Coll, frightened, backs down ... Then Maris steps in, makes a speech about how everything is going to fall apart if they keep giving the wings to bad flyers, about how it's people like Woodwings who should be given the right to fly, not people like Raven (we work in both stories), etc. Coll takes heart from her stand – he stands up and gives her the wings, renounces them, defies his father.

Suggestion: we can use Coll's speech from *my* original ending in the sand-candle scene, and his renunciation from *your* ending in this landing beach scene. This is the Law of Conservation of Prose And Avoidal of Rewriting.

Going on to outline (in two more single-spaced pages) the story we could write, George concluded happily:

This way the story becomes so incredibly tight ... All those lovely songs ... become important. Garth and Dorrel and Barrion all advance the plot substantially, but Maris is the heroine, Maris solves the problem. We've hardly got a loose end left.

And nearly no rewriting – just about everything we have now is prime stuff that we can keep. A lot of new writing to do, of course, but I'm enthusiastic about that now, and I hope you are, too. Instead of chewing up the story like used gum ...we get a better, longer story ...

As for the title, George suggested – and I approved – 'The Winds of Change'. But when Ben Bova bought it for *Analog* he renamed it 'The Storms of Windhaven' – which we had to agree was even better. Ben also came up with the perfect quote for an epigraph:

'For once you have tasted flight you will walk the earth with your eyes turned skyward; for there you have been, and there you long to return.'

Leonardo Da Vinci

It's a quotation that I think applies to fiction writing quite as much as to flying.

A few last words

This has been a very personal, autobiographical book to write. Although I've read a lot of books about writing, and worked with a number of writers over the years (as friend, collaborator, student, teacher and editor), and listened to and learned from many others, ultimately the only advice I can give about writing comes from my own experience. I hope at least some of it will be useful to you. Good luck on finding your own way.

Useful Addresses

Ansible ('SF News and Gossip')
www.dcs.gla.ac.uk/Ansible

Arvon Foundation
www.arvonfoundation.org
Totleigh Barton
Sheepwash
Beaworthy
Devon EX21 5NS

British Fantasy Society
www.britishfantasysociety.com

British Science Fiction Society
www.bsfa.co.uk
Estelle Roberts, Membership Secretary
97 Sharp Street
Newland Avenue
Hull HU5 2AE

Clarion West
www.clarionwest.org/website
340 Fifteenth Avenue East
Suite 350
Seattle WA 98112
USA

Directory of Writers' Circles
www.writers-circles.com
Diana Hayden
39 Lincoln Way
Harlington
Beds LU5 6NG

Locus ('The Magazine of the Science Fiction & Fantasy Field')
www.locusmag.com
Locus Publications
PO Box 13305
Oakland CA 94661
USA

Science Fiction and Fantasy Writers of America (SFWA)
www.sfwa.org/

Ty Newydd Writers' Centre
www.tynewydd.org
Llanystumdwy
Cricieth
Gwynedd LL52 OLW

Acknowledgements

Dunsany, Lord, *The King of Elfland's Daughter* © Lord Dunsany 1924; renewed 1951. Used by permission of Victor Gollancz, a division of The Orion Publishing Group. Pages 89–90.

Harlan Ellison is quoted by Samuel R. Delany in *The Jewel-Hinged Jaw* (Dragon Press, 1977), page 54.

John Gardner is quoted in *Advice to Writers*, ed. Jon Winokur (Vintage, 2000), pages 59–60.

Gibson, William, *Neuromancer* © William Gibson 1984. Used by permission of the author and Berkley Publishing Group, a division of Penguin Group (USA) Inc. (Ace, 1984), pages 56–57.

The extracts from *The Reader Over Your Shoulder* by Robert Graves and Alan Hodge are quoted in *Advice to Writers*, ed. Jon Winokur (Vintage, 2000), page 107.

Jones, Gwyneth, 'Characters and how they grow', first published in *Focus*, Issue 24, June/July 1993, by permission of the author, pages 64, 68–9.

LeGuin, Ursula K., *The Dispossessed* © 1974 Ursula K. LeGuin. Reprinted by permission of HarperCollins Publishers Inc., pages 83–84.

Russ, Joanna, 'On Setting', from *Those Who Can: A Science Fiction Reader*, ed. Robin Scott Wilson (New American Library, 1974), page 52.

Schweitzer, Darrell, from a review published in *The New York Review of Science Fiction*, November 2000, page 116.

Stableford, Brian, *The Way to Write Science Fiction* (Elm Tree Books, 1989), page 95.

Waldrop, Howard, *Night of the Cooters* (Ursus, 1990), pages 45–46, by permission of the author.

Every effort has been made to trace and acknowledge copyright-owners. If any right has been omitted, the publishers offer their apologies and will rectify this in subsequent editions following notification.

Bibliography

Aldiss, Brian W. with Wingrove, David, *Trillion Year Spree* (Gollancz, 1986)

Atwood, Margaret, *Oryx and Crake* (Bloomsbury, 2003)

Boyer, Robert H. & Zahorski, K., eds., *Fantasists on Fantasy* (Avon, 1984)

Clute, John, *Appleseed* (Orbit, 2001)

Clute, John & Grant, John, eds., *The Encyclopedia of Fantasy* (Orbit, 1997)

Clute, John & Nicholls, Peter, eds., *The Encyclopedia of Science Fiction* (Orbit, 1993)

Danielewski, Mark Z., *House of Leaves* (Doubleday, 2000)

Delany, Samuel R., *The Jewel-Hinged Jaw* (Dragon Press, 1977)

Dunsany, Lord, *The King of Elfland's Daughter* (Gollancz, 2001)

Gabaldon, Diana, *Cross-Stitch* (Century, 1991)

Garner, Alan, *The Voice That Thunders* (Harvill Press, 1997); *The Owl Service* (Collins, 1998)

Gentle, Mary, *Ash: A Secret History* (Gollancz, 2000)

Gibson, William, *Neuromancer* (Ace, 1984)

Holdstock, Robert, *Mythago Wood* (Gollancz, 1984)

Jones, Diana Wynne, *The Tough Guide to Fantasyland* (Vista, 1996)

King, Stephen, *On Writing: A Memoir of the Craft* (Hodder & Stoughton, 2000)

Klein, Rachel, *The Moth Diaries* (Faber, 2004)

Koontz, Dean, *How To Write Best-Selling Fiction* (Writers Digest Books, 1981)

LeGuin, Ursula K., *The Dispossessed* (Harper & Row, 1974); *The Language of the Night* (Putnam, 1979); *Steering the Craft* (Eighth Mountain Press, 1998)

Martin, George R. R., *A Game of Thrones* (Bantam Books, 1996)

Martin, George R. R. & Tuttle, Lisa, *Windhaven* (Millennium, 2000)

Mieville, China, *Perdido Street Station* (Macmillan, 2000)

Nicholls, Stan, *Wordsmiths of Wonder: Fifty Interviews with Writers of the Fantastic* (Orbit, 1993)

Niffenegger, Audrey, *The Time Traveller's Wife* (Jonathan Cape, 2004)

Pullman, Philip, 'His Dark Materials' trilogy, comprising: *Northern Lights*, *The Subtle Knife* and *The Amber Spyglass* (Scholastic, 2001)

Reynolds, Alistair, *Revelation Space* (Gollancz, 2000)

Roberts, Nora, *Key of Light* (Piatkus, 2003)

Robinson, Kim Stanley, *The Years of Rice and Salt* (Harper-Collins, 2003)

Rowling, J. K., *Harry Potter and the Philosopher's Stone* (Bloomsbury, 1996)

Russ, Joanna, *We Who Are About To ...* (The Women's Press, 1987)

Shapiro, Marc, *J. K. Rowling: The Wizard Behind Harry Potter* (St Martin's Press, 2000)

Stableford, Brian, *The Way to Write Science Fiction* (Elm Tree Books, 1989)

Strunk, William Jr. & White, E. B., *The Elements of Style* (Longman, 1999)

Tolkien, J. R. R., *The Lord of the Rings* (HarperCollins, 1995)

Tuttle, Lisa, *Mad House* (Mammoth, 1998); *Panther in Argyll* (Mammoth, 2000); *Lost Futures* (Grafton, 1992)

Waggoner, Diana, *The Hills of Faraway: A Guide to Fantasy* (Atheneum, 1978)

Waldrop, Howard, *All About Strange Monsters of the Recent Past: Neat Stories* (Ursus, 1987); *Night of the Cooters: More Neat Stories* (Ursus; Ziesing, 1990); *Going Home Again* (St Martin's Press, 1997)

Wilson, Robin Scott, ed., *Those Who Can: A Science Fiction Reader* (New American Library, 1974)

Winokur, Jon, ed., *Advice to Writers* (Vintage, 2000)

Index

'Family Monkey, The' 23–4, 118
fandom 141–2
Fletcher, Jo 155–163
foreshadowing 105
'From Elfland to Poughkeepsie' 88, 90–1

Gabaldon, Diana 13, 15, 79
Gabriel 86–7
Gaiman, Neil 14
Gardner, John 59
Garner, Alan 29, 48, 131–2
Gentle, Mary 3, 7, 16, 45
Gibson, William 7, 20–1, 55–7, 152
ghost stories 112, 119
grammar and punctuation 106–7

Harris, Joanne 1
Harry Potter 9, 15, 129, 131–2, 136
Harwood, Antony 50, 149
Heinlein, Robert 22, 54, 59, 123, 128
heroic fantasy 2, 11, 89–90
Holdstock, Robert 29, 48, 51
Holman, Tim 155–162
humour 12, 121

ideas 19–25, 31–4, 36–7, 121
idiot plot 63, 75
imaginary worlds 37–8
info-dumps 95–6

James, Henry 33, 35, 64, 79
Johnson, Jane 155–162
Jones, Diana Wynne 50, 133
Jones, Gwyneth 64, 68–9, 111

King of Elfland's Daughter, The 89–90
King, Stephen 61, 70, 98, 148, 152, 154
Kilworth, Garry 31, 48, 144
Koontz, Dean 24, 83, 137

landscape 35–6, 48–53
Lavery, Peter 155–62
LeGuin, Ursula 2, 8, 20, 25, 68, 83, 88, 90, 108, 130, 131
Lord of the Rings, The 9–11, 17, 48, 51
Lost Futures 7, 41, 44, 65, 66

Mad House 24, 137–8
manuscript format 149–50
lengths 16–8, 102–3, 115–8
maps 50–1
markets 124–5, 130, 142
Martin, George R.R. 12, 15, 16, 38, 47, 86, 99, 139, 154, 164–177
Mieville, China 2, 7, 38
Murray, Colin 4
Mythago Wood 29, 48, 51